I0088333

Saving the Celtics

A Be the General Manager Book

Bryant T. Jordan

Sports Seer Publishing

Saving the Celtics: A Be the General Manager Book

© Copyright 2014 by Bryant T. Jordan

All rights reserved. No portion of this book may be reproduced in any form without prior written permission of the author.

All sports celebrity quotes in this book come from **www.brainyquote.com**. Copyright 2001 - 2014 BrainyQuote.

Published by Sports Seer Publishing

Library and Archives Canada Cataloguing in Publication

Jordan, Bryant T., 1979-, author

    Saving the Celtics : a be the General Manager book / Bryant T. Jordan.

Issued in print and electronic formats.

ISBN 978-1-927654-26-2 (bound).--ISBN 978-1-927654-27-9 (pbk.)

ISBN 978-1-927654-28-6 (pdf)

    1. Boston Celtics (Basketball team). 2. Basketball teams--United States--Management. 3. Basketball managers--United States. I. Title.

GV885.52.B67J66 2014   796.323'64097446   C2014-902603-X

                            C2014-902604-8

Publisher: **www.SportsSeerPublishing.com**

First Book: **www.SavingTheLakers.com**

Second Book: **www.SavingTheCeltics.com**

Author: **www.BryantTJordan.com**

Dedicated to God: Father, Word and Holy Spirit

Also by Bryant T. Jordan

Saving the Lakers: A Be the General Manager Book
www.SavingTheLakers.com

An Open Letter to ALL Regarding Donald Sterling
www.bryantTjordan.com/donald-sterling-book/

A winner is someone who recognizes his God-given talents, works his tail off to develop them into skills, and uses these skills to accomplish his goals.

-Larry Bird

He who believes in nobody knows that he himself is not to be trusted.

- Red Auerbach

Most people have a harder time letting themselves love than finding someone to love them.

- Bill Russell

ACKNOWLEDGEMENTS

First and foremost I want to thank my first love, God the Father, Word and Holy Spirit. Without Him I am nothing.

I would also like to thank all the great NCAA and NBA ballers I grew up watching. You were each an inspiration to a knucklehead who could be dead or in prison if it weren't for the fact that I spent most of my waking hours either hooping or safely watching basketball games in my room, rather than runnin' around Shaqtin' a fool.

Last but certainly not least I would like to thank my magnificent wife and our precious children; words cannot express how thankful I am to have been blessed with each and every one of you and how very much I love you. May you each serve God above all and always do what you believe is right, no matter what anyone else thinks, says, or does!

CONTENTS

PROLOGUE

How Saving the Lakers: A Be the General Manager Book turned into Saving the Celtics: A Be the General Manager Book

Long, long ago, in the spring of 2014, destiny struck. I had just finished my umpteenth draft of Saving the Lakers: A Be the General Manager Book and the idea to use that as a base from which to write this book entered my mind.

I descended the main staircase that leads from my writing quarters to our sitting room and entered the kitchen, where my amazing wife, as usual, was preparing something for one or more of our children. I told her about the idea that entered my mind. She seemed to both think I was crazy and that such an idea made perfect sense. I felt the exact same way.

Saving the Lakers: A Be the General Manager Book had both been a joy to write and an absolute nightmare and headache to endure. I had started writing the book before the 2013-14 season began, before Kobe Bryant signed his two-year, $48,500,000 contract, before he had subsequently re-injured himself and missed almost the entire season, before the Lakers had failed to trade Steve Nash at the trade deadline, even before the team became one of the laughing stocks of the entire NBA.

My first draft of Saving the Lakers had the opportunity to negotiate Kobe Bryant's next contract as one of the Choose Your Own Adventure style options built into it. My next draft factored in the Lakers making the Playoffs and therefore having the options of drafting such players as Andrew Harrison, Jahii Carson and others, rather than the top 10 talent pool they will be choosing from now. These drafts and revisions kept coming and coming and I felt like the book would never get written more than once.

Even now, as I type this introduction, I am not entirely finished with Saving the Lakers. At present I have them receiving the fifth pick in the draft, however depending on how the May 20th NBA Draft Lottery unfolds, things could change dramatically and an entirely new version of the book may need to be written.

This is literally the most challenging writing project I have even undertaken and that includes the sestina I wrote during my college years and the various Christian works I have authored under various pennames throughout the years. Literally, I would not wish writing this sort of book on my worst enemy. The problem is not so much that the subject matter is difficult or that the math is too advanced, but merely that the deadlines are problematic in the extreme.

Considering these books (Saving the Lakers and Saving the Celtics) can only be published after the Draft Lottery on May 20, 2013, but before the actual NBA Draft on June 27, 2013, which takes place a mere 31 days later, the timing of this endeavor is absolutely maddening. Basically I will need to re-write these books and create the final version within 48 hours of the Draft Lottery ending, get them off to my publisher for some quick editing and formatting, and then simply hope that everything is done and ready for a June 1, 2014 publication date.

That said, I had hoped to be able to publish this through one of the major publishers, receive a sizeable advance and merely reap the rewards of my work, rather than share in the risk publishing has become. However, I wasn't able to find a single major publisher who could work under such extreme deadlines. A typical publisher plans months, if not more than a year ahead, so to contact one and ask them if they could have a book published and ready to be ordered by the public a mere nine days or so after receiving the final draft is just absurd.

Regardless, I am dedicated to making these books a reality, and am sincerely praying that God's will be done. He has lead me through some of the most insane and trying experiences in the past and I trust Him to do so again with this minor dilemma this time around.

INTRODUCTION

I have always been a jock but perhaps even more so a stats-geek and money-man. Ever since I was extremely young I have been a bit of a walking calculator, able to do many mathematical equations in my head faster than another can do with a calculator at his or her disposal. When I became interested in sports, it was only natural that I would instantly also become interested in player's salaries, team salary constraints and the like.

After I basically hung up my high-tops for good in order to give my ankles, knees and back a break, the financial side of the game invaded my mind even more. When websites like RealGM.com and HoopsHype.com with its team salary pages came on-line, I was in arm-chair GM heaven. I quickly memorized the salaries of perhaps over 100 players and began constructing trades in my head and on-paper to improve every team in the league. I also started writing on various websites and forums which almost always led to my being kicked off the site by some overzealous moderator or cyber-Nazi who happened to disagree with my opinions on his or her favorite team's problems and how to fix them with a trade that made both basketball and financial sense. Such is life.

No matter, when the urge to write a trade proposal crept up I simply searched the web for another website, and of course, used a separate pseudonym. I even ran my own sports blog for a short time until I realized that I just didn't have enough time to dedicate to it, with all the other family, ministry and writing projects I was involved in. However when the 2012-13 season ended, I was a bit burned out. Life was happening, our ninth child was on the way, my family and I were planning a cross country relocation and I simply disappeared from the forums and websites I had once so passionately haunted.

Life is still happening and now just eight months after relocating and getting all settled in we are once again in an entirely different locale (after yet another long and strenuous relocation), this time settling into a recently purchased home we would like to actually live in for more than 12 months.

However, although life is still as unpredictable as ever, the 2013-14 NBA season is almost finished, the Boston Celtics are an enigma after trading franchise savior's Paul Pierce and Kevin Garnett and signing a coach who looks like he could be playing ball on my 14 year old son's team in Brad Stevens (a great hire in my mind by the way), and, most importantly, the Celtics have the pieces necessary (expiring contracts, cap space, draft picks and talented tradeable players) to build an NBA championship level roster in short order. At a time like this, how could I not write about the Celtics?

As for where the idea for a Be the General Manager and Choose your Own Ending Sports Adventure book came from, such is an easy question to answer. My children and even I myself have always enjoyed Choose Your Own Adventure books and I have been the quintessential arm-chair General Manager for years now; simply put, I was bound to write a book like this someday. And, with the Celtics having the necessary pieces to recreate their entire team and turn one of the worst teams in 2013-14 into one of the best teams in 2014-15 I thought now was the perfect time to write this book. Of course, it also made perfect sense to write this book after having recently finished Saving the Lakers: A Be the General Manager Book, so there's that too.

Anyways, my hope is that young and old Celtics fans, stat-geeks, number-crunchers, arm-chair GM's and just plain basketball fans alike will enjoy this book and read it again and again and again, until they make all the correct choices necessary to win the championship. The truth is that winning the title on one's first read-through of this book is much, much, much harder to do than winning the NBA title is for any player in the league today, period.

There are only 30 teams in the league which means that every team starts the season with a 1-in-30 chance of winning the title or 30/1 odds. However, in order to win the championship in this book, you will have to beat incredible odds. How incredible you ask? Simply put, you literally have a better chance of actually playing in the NBA than you have of winning the title on your first read-through of this book; yes, I'm serious!

The odds that you win the title on your first read through of this book are exactly 995,330 / 1. That's right nine- hundred and ninty-five thousand, three-hundred and thirty to one! You literally have a .00000100469 percent chance of winning the title on your first read through of this book!

Simply put, there are about 80 countries on the face of planet earth whose entire populations could read and try to win the title on their first read through of this book without even one single citizen doing so. In the good ole U.S.A, if every single one of its 317,000,000 citizens, including the comatose, infants and Otis Smith, read this book, a whopping 318 people would be able to win the title on their first read-through. In comparison there are well over 500 players and coaches in the NBA today. Think about that. No seriously, really think about that; it's insane!

If you can conquer this book and win the title on your first, or even your tenth read-through, you could be a real life NBA General Manager one day. I honestly believe that, especially considering Otis Smith was once hired as a General Manager. All of that said, read carefully, chose wisely, stay true to who you are, make the decisions you feel will help the team win the 2014-15 NBA title … and don't forget to have fun!

PREPARATION MAKES PERFECT

So you want to run the Boston Celtics, eh? You want to be the General Manager of the most popular, beloved and hated professional sports franchise on the planet, eh? Then you better prepare yourself like never before!

You will only get one shot at impressing Celtics Managing Partner, Governor and Chief Executive Officer (CEO) Wyc Grousbeck. After just one meeting you will either be hired or forgotten, you will either be leading one of the two greatest franchises in the history of the NBA or looking for work as a grade school girls basketball coach thinking about what could have been.

You've probably seen the fictional Hollywood movie Eddie starring Whoopi Goldberg, about a New York Knicks fan who amazingly ends up becoming coach of her favorite team. You've also probably heard the true story of the grocery bagger who became the starting QB of the St. Louis Rams and led the Greatest Show on Turf to a Super Bowl victory over the Tennessee Titans. The fact is that truth is literally stranger than fiction and amazing things do indeed happen every day in real life even if the majority of the masses are too jaded and desensitized to recognize such glimpses of the divine.

The fact is also that the Boston Celtics just finished their worst season since the 2006-07 campaign when they won just 24 games and there is no better time for change than the present, especially in the title-hungry City of Champions that is Boston! And, you know what happened the year after 2006-07 right? The Celtics landed Kevin Garnett and Ray Allen and won the NBA title!

Celtics CEO Wyc Grousbeck has decided that Danny Ainge is no longer capable of functioning as both President of Basketball Operations and de facto General Manager. This said, Grousbeck has decided to hire a new General Manger and to have such in place before the NBA draft. If you play your cards right, that new General Manager will be you!

You have exactly one week to prepare yourself for your interview with CEO Grousbeck. You have just one week to have a plan in place that you can present to Mr. Grousbeck, a plan that will not only demonstrate your remarkable understanding of the players currently under contract and those who could be signed, but of the potential draftees and how they would fit into your plans for the upcoming season, and of the available free agents and which ones you will be focused on signing to contracts. Most importantly, you have just one week to figure out how you will convince CEO Grousbeck that you are the individual to lead the Boston Celtics to the 2015 NBA title!

The internet is filled with a host of wonderful websites which you should familiarize yourself with as soon and as often as possible. From studying team and player salaries at HoopsHype.com, to understanding the NBA's collective Bargaining Agreement and financial aspect of completing an NBA trade at Larry Coon's CBAFAQ.com, to considering various fan-inspired trade possibilities on RealGm.com, preparation will be paramount. From getting a feel for the Celtics fans expectations at CelticsBlog.com, to possibly stealing a few solid ideas for how the team should proceed on draft day at BleacherReport.com, to studying the profiles of potential draft prospects at such excellent sites as draftexpress.com and nbadraft.net, you need to buckle down and prepare to read, study and think more than you have since you crammed for that high school algebra test.

You may also want to familiarize yourself with what professional sports writers, ex-players and the like feel the Celtics need to do to improve by browsing such sites as sports.yahoo.com/nba, msn.foxsports.com/nba and of course NBA.com!

You have your work cut out for you but no matter your age or credentials, if you prepare yourself for success and deliver a plan that blows Wyc Grousbeck's socks off, the job will be yours for the taking!

YOUR INTERVIEW WITH WYC GROUSBECK

Celtics CEO Wyc Grousbeck: *Hello, my name's Wyc Grousbeck and I am the owner of the greatest professional sports team on the planet, a team you obviously want to be the General Manager of. Allow me to be blunt, I don't know you, your credentials are lacking, and frankly at this point I have no idea why I should hire you when I could hire one of the greatest players of all-time who would kill for a chance to run the Celtics such as Charles Barkley, or even an ex-Celtic with multiple rings like Sam Cassell.*

However, I believe in giving people a chance and I did read the report you emailed me and was impressed; it's obvious you prepared well and have a solid plan for the future. I'm going to give you a chance to prove to me that you're the man that will return this great franchise to glory.

have already interviewed Charles Barkley as well as a few other choice candidates including former Celtic and three-time champion Sam Cassell, TNT analyst Kenny Smith, and of course former Celtic, the 'Ginger Ninja', the 'White Mamba', Brian Scalabrine, because, well, he's Brian Scalabrine! However, truth be told, only Sam Cassell impressed me.

Kenny Smith kept ranting on and on about how his Rockets teams would have beaten the Bulls in the Finals had Jordan never retired. Barkley threatened to throw me through a window if I hired Kenny Smith over him. And Brian Scalabrine actually said the job wasn't worthy of his unique gifts. He literally told me that since Golden State Warriors Coach Mark Jackson demoted him to the Santa Cruz Warriors in the D-League for arguing with fellow Warriors Assistant Coach Pete Myers, he had realized that his mission in life was to help equip D-Leaguers to be as dominant in the NBA one day as he was. Scalabrine dreams of being able to help even one D-League player average 3.1 points and shoot .390 in the NBA like he did over his illustrious career, so, I guess, more power to him.

All of the above said, the fact is I am going to hire Sam Cassell if you don't impress me more than he did. Sam may not have been the greatest player that has ever worn the green and white but he was clutch throughout his career and the epitome of a 'winner'. I mean, come on, the guy won three rings with two different teams, including our last one as a franchise in 2007-08, and came close to winning two more with two other teams (Milwaukee in 2001 and Minnesota in 2004). He was also quite a player in his day and racked up over 17,000 points and 6,000 assists in his career if you include the playoffs. The guy has also been an Assistant Coach for the Wizards recently and has done a great job with John Wall and Bradley Beal and I think he deserves a shot at this position.

I'll get right to the point; if you can answer each of the following four questions correctly I will offer you a contract on the spot as Cassell only answered three correctly. If you can't, you can root for the Celtics from your sofa.

Question One: If you could start next season with a prime Rajon Rondo or a prime Kobe Bryant, which player would you choose?

If your answer to Question One is Magic Johnson, turn to page 24.

If your answer to Question One is Rajon Rondo, turn to page 25.

Celtics CEO Wyc Grousbeck: *Good job, I would have thrown you out of my office had you said you'd build a team around a prime Rondo over a prime Magic simply out of loyalty to Celtics players. If I hire you need to be loyal to this team, not its players. You draft, sign and trade for the best players available, period.*

Continue on to page 26.

Celtics CEO Wyc Grousbeck: *Get out of my office or I'll throw you out! I love Rondo as much as anyone but only an idiot would choose to build a team around Rondo instead of Magic Johnson. Rondo's best season ever saw him average 13.7 points, 11.1 assists, 5.6 rebounds career and 1.8 steals per game. Magic Johnson 'averaged' more points, assists, rebounds, assists and steals throughout his entire 13 year career.*

Magic was just a born leader, a born winner and his teammates loved him. Rondo's great but Magic was other-worldly, even if he did play for the Lakers!

You're journey has ended.
Enjoy being an armchair GM.

Words of Wisdom:

Leadership is diving for a loose ball, getting the crowd involved, getting other players involved. It's being able to take it as well as dish it out. That's the only way you're going to get respect from the players.

-Larry Bird

Celtics CEO Wyc Grousbeck: *Nice job answering the first question. However, Sam Cassell also answered that question correctly. It's time for your second question.*

Question Two: Who would you rather have shooting a wide open three pointer with the game on the line in their prime, Bob Cousy or Steve Kerr?

If your answer to Question Two is Bob Cousy,
turn to page 27.

If your answer to Question Two is Steve Kerr,
turn to page 28.

Celtics CEO Wyc Grousbeck: *Have you ever considered a career as a stand-up comedian? Bob Cousy may have been one of the greatest guards in league history and a Celtics legend but that doesn't mean he was one of the best in every single facet of the game. If you'd really rather have a player who shot an abysmal .375 from the floor and had no range on his jump-shot, taking the final shot instead of one of the best pure shooters the game has ever seen, a guy who averaged better than .500 on three-pointers in four different seasons and a guy who shot .454 from distance over his entire career, logic isn't your strong point.*

I simply can't trust you to build a true title-contenting roster if you can't even comprehend that players have different roles on a basketball team. It's time to go home and start rehearsing your bit funny man.

You're journey has ended.

Enjoy being an armchair GM.

Words of Wisdom:

Just do what you do best.

-Red Aeurbach

Celtics CEO Wyc Grousbeck: *Great answer! I was sure you'd get that question wrong; great answer! There aren't too many people that think rationally enough to know the best option is not always the best player. I'm impressed, however don't too excited, Sam Cassell answered this question correctly as well and if there's a tie I'm going to hire the former Celtic, no offense.*

Continue on to page 29.

Celtics CEO Wyc Grousbeck: *You're two for two; nice work! Of course Sam Cassell answered the first two questions correctly as well so you've still got a lot of work to do. It's time for the third question.*

Question Three: Would you ever advocate tanking (i.e. losing games on purpose) in order to improve your team's draft position?

**If your answer to Question Three is yes,
turn to page 30.**

**If your answer to Question Two is no,
turn to page 31.**

Celtics CEO Wyc Grousbeck: *Oh baby, now you're talking! I can't believe you got that one right. Of course, I couldn't believe Sam Cassell got that one right either but he did.*

Most fans see nothing wrong with a team purposely losing one or two games towards the end of the season in order to position themselves for the playoffs and give themselves the best matchup possible, yet those same fans feel it's wrong and even cheating to tank for an entire season in order to give oneself the best chance at receiving the highest draft pick possible. That's hypocritical in my book. Every Owner, General Manager and Coach is supposed to do what's best for the team, not for the league, not for the fans, but for the team and sometimes tanking is what's best, period.

Continue on to page 32.

Celtics CEO Wyc Grousbeck: *You almost made it but you blew it. I understand you may have thought I would congratulate you on saying you'd never advocate tanking, call you a high-character individual and say you're the sort of General I want leading the Celtics into battle, but you'd be mistaken.*

Whether it's losing a game at the end of the year to make sure your team gets a more favorable matchup in the first round of the playoffs, or losing a great many games to make sure your team has the best chance of landing the highest possible lottery pick it can, tanking is a necessity at times. Anyone qualified to be an NBA General Manager would know that. Get out of my office!

You're journey has ended.
Enjoy being an armchair GM.

Words of Wisdom:

That's what makes it so fun to be on a team. You're sitting at your house, thinking up this wild, crazy stuff as to how it's going to go, and the other guys are sitting at their houses doing the same thing.

- Bill Walton

Celtics CEO Wyc Grousbeck: *Great job; you're three for three! Sam Cassell was also three for three though so don't get too cocky.*

It all comes down to this final question. If you answer it correctly I will happily offer you a contract as Sam Cassell did not answer this fourth question to my satisfaction. However, if you answer this question incorrectly I will hire Cassell. It's as simple as that.

Question Four: Would you ever trade or release a fan favorite or even a team legend that happens to have a bad contract or no valid role on the team going forward?

**If your answer to Question Four is yes,
turn to page 33.**

**If your answer to Question Four is no,
turn to page 34.**

Celtics CEO Wyc Grousbeck: *Are you kidding me; are you kidding me right now? You did it; you actually did it!*

That was the one and only question Sam Cassell answered incorrectly and I'm pretty sure I know why. You see, Cassell was traded seven times in his career, seven! He won back-to-back titles with the Rockets and then got traded just a year later. In fact, we even traded him for nothing more than a second round pick after he helped us win our last title in 2008.

I'm sure that hurt Sam and when I asked him the fourth question he allowed such personal hurt to cloud his judgment. He answered with emotion instead of logic and it cost him this job. However you answered every question correctly; amazing!

Congratulations, the job is yours and I'll make sure a contract is in your hands by tomorrow afternoon. Enjoy tonight, your dream is about to come true!

Continue on to page 35.

Celtics CEO Wyc Grousbeck: *I had such high hopes for you but you blew it. No individual player is above the team and any great GM knows that. Sam Cassell also got this question wrong but as I said before, if this little contest of mine ends in a tie, the job would go to the former Celtic and I am a man of my word. Goodbye.*

You're journey has ended.
Enjoy being an armchair GM.

Words of Wisdom:

Basketball is one of those rare opportunities where you can make a difference, not only for yourself, but for other people as well.

-Bill Walton

THE OFFER

Celtics CEO Wyc Grousbeck: *Today is the day, the day you get to put pen to paper and become the newest General Manager of the Boston Celtics! Today is the day you get to follow in the footsteps of all the Celtics greats and create your own unforgettable legacy!*

I am offering you a one year contract with a base salary of just $500,000 but with a $1,500,000 bonus due upon winning the NBA title, along with a three year option worth an additional $6,000,000 that you can opt into if we win the title this year. However, understand that there are no guarantees with this contract; if you fail to lead us to an NBA title in your very first year you will be fired.

So, what is your decision?

Decision One: Accept the contract as-is.

Decision Two: Ask for a guaranteed salary of $1,000,000 in the first year knowing that such is still below market value for such a high profile position within one of the wealthiest organizations in the league.

Decision Three: Ask for a guaranteed second year rather than a mere one year contract while making it clear that you will function better with added security which will in turn benefit the team.

If you chose Decision One, turn to page 36.

If you chose Decision Two, turn to page 37.

If you chose Decision Three, turn to page 38.

Celtics CEO Wyc Grousbeck: *Welcome to the Celtics! You have an enormous amount of work ahead of you and you better be prepared to make tough decisions and take no prisoners. The NBA Draft is right around the corner with free agency following. I'd like you to build the roster as you see fit, draft who you like, trade who you like, and sign who you want; I won't interfere and money is no object.*

Congratulations. Now get to work and bring home that trophy!

Continue on to page 39.

Celtics CEO Wyc Grousbeck: *You greedy little punk. I offer you the keys to the kingdom and you demand more money? You disappoint me. My offer is off the table and Sam Cassell will be the next General Manager of the Celtics. Get out!*

You're journey has ended.
Enjoy being an armchair GM.

Words of Wisdom:

I really don't like talking about money. All I can say is that the Good Lord must have wanted me to have it.

- Larry Bird

Celtics CEO Wyc Grousbeck: *You blew a chance to become the General Manager of the greatest team in NBA history simply because you were greedy for a second year that may never even have come. You haven't proven anything, haven't put in one solid day's work and yet you demand a second year? Get out of my office and have fun watching A.C. Green get the dream job you could have had!*

You're journey has ended.
Enjoy being an armchair GM.

Words of Wisdom:

An acre of performance is worth a whole world of promise.

- Red Aeurbach

DRAFT DAY

After signing your one year, win-a-ring-or-bust contract, you immediately went to work preparing for the draft, a draft that some consider to be the deepest since the 1996 NBA Draft which was perhaps the greatest draft ever. During the 96' Draft Kobe Bryant himself lasted until the 13th pick! Future *Hall of Famers* Steve Nash, Allen Iverson and Ray Allen were also selected in that legendary draft, not to mention All-Star level and standout performers such as Stephon Marbury, Antoine Walker, Jermaine O'Neal, Shareef Abdur-Rahim, Marcus Camby, Peja Stojakovic and Zydrunas Ilgauskas. There was even an undrafted rookie that year who turned out to be one of the greatest defensive players the league has ever seen by the name of Ben Wallace, and of course that is the year we drafted Antoine Walker as well, a player whose career is vastly under-rated. Walker was an absolute monster his first seven years in the league and CEO Grousbeck still cringes whenever he thinks about the team trading him for the Mavericks garbage on October 20, 2003. He will never forget that date and if you ever make a trade like that he will personally see to it that the only job you can get in basketball is as a hot-dog salesman for a D-League affiliate!

Without a second round pick in this year's draft (the Dallas Mavericks own the Celtics pick) you are able to focus on making just two first round selections, your own as well as the Nets selection, two selections that could end up defining or destroying your entire career. After watching the Ping-Pong balls bounce and seeing your team receive the 6th pick in the 2014 NBA draft you realized the pressure was on. The Celtics are not the sort of team that finds themselves in the draft lottery very often and when they do, the fans don't expect mere professionalism, they expect perfection.

2014 will be the first time in seven years the Celtics have a lottery pick. Again, Celtics fans expect perfection; you better make this pick count!

You watched Kansas center Joel Embiid get selected with the number one overall pick by the Cleveland Cavaliers, while wondering to yourself whether he will turn out to be more Hakeem Olajuwon than Michael Olowokandi. You quietly rejoiced that you didn't have to take that risk.

Next you heard Andrew Wiggins named called and shook your head. You aren't sure if he'll be the next LeBron James or merely the next Tracy McGrady but you know for a fact you would have been happy drafting the next Tracy McGrady and would have jumped at the chance to draft Wiggins.

Duke small forward Jabari Parker was selected third by the Philadelphia 76'3ers. You liked Parker's game and felt he could have been a solid young man to build around for the future; however you're not crushed that you missed out on drafting the former *Blue Devil* with the polished offensive game. Considering that Parker could one day disappear for a couple of years on a Mormon mission and the fact that you see more Carmelo Anthony (i.e. mostly offense with very little defense) in his game than you'd like to see, you smile to yourself.

With the fourth pick in the draft the Orlando Magic selected Marcus Smart, the 6'4", 225 lb., 20 year old combo guard from Oklahoma State University with the rough and rugged game is now off the board. You aren't sure you would have drafted Smart with the 6th pick but he certainly would have received strong consideration, especially due to his reputation as an absolute terror on the defensive end.

When the name of the fifth pick is called you almost let out a scream of sheer delight. Noah Vonleh, the 6'9", 247 lb. big man from Indiana was just drafted by the Utah Jazz, a shocking pick. There is a reason bad teams are bad teams.

After what seemed like an eternity of waiting, you hear new NBA Commissioner Adam Silver declare, *the Boston Celtics are now on the clock*. There are three players still on the board that you have a very sincere interest in:

Dante Exum: This 6'6, 188 lb., 18 year old combo guard from Australia is a silky smooth athlete that has the tools to be effective at either guard position. He also has the potential to be a strong defender as well, thanks in large part to his 6' 9.25" wingspan.

Exum is considered a bit of a Penny Hardaway clone by some and is known for his extreme fluidity and body control, great first step and open-court mastery. He also comes from solid stock with his father Cecil having played for the University of North Carolina Tar Heels 1982 championship team (the same team that featured James Worthy and a freshman named Michael Jordan).

Dante himself has also proven to be a winner, leading Lake Ginninderra College to the *Australian National Schools Basketball Title*, not to mention leading the World Select Team to a victory of the USA Junior Select Team during the *2013 Nike Hoop Summit*.

There are some concerns with Exum however. His jump-shot is anything but automatic due to poor mechanics. He also has a very slight frame and may have a hard time scoring, or even creating separation for himself, against the grown men that will be guarding him in the NBA. However, perhaps the biggest concern is Exum's age, inexperience and the level of competition he faced in Australia. He simply may not be ready to be a dependable contributor on a contending team for at least 3-4 years.

Julius Randle: This 6'9", 248 lb., 19 year old power forward with the non-stop motor and bruising style of play that reminds you of a cross between Zach Randolph and Blake Griffin (or even Dominique Wilkins and Anthony Mason as strange as that sounds) won three *Texas High School State Championships* in four years before playing like a man among boys during his freshman season at the University of Kentucky. From his very first week on campus when he averaged 24 points while shooting over 61% from the floor and hauled in 14.3 rebounds while playing just 30 minutes per game, Randle was a monster!

Randle has all the skills a power forward needs to play at an extremely high level in the NBA. He has great footwork, can score both with his back to the basket in the post and facing up from the perimeter. He also has great explosiveness and is a nightmare for opposing defenses when running the court in transition. He's also known to be an incredibly hard worker and someone that elevates his teammates play through his sheer aggressiveness and enormous competitive spirit.

The only real knocks on Randle's game are that he is a bit turnover prone (though the same can be said for many freshman power forwards) and seems to rely on bullying his opponent to get buckets which may not be possible against bigger, stronger and better athletes at the next level. However, you're not so sure about the last point as while Randle may have a hard time scoring against the likes of Anthony Davis at the next level, there is only one Anthony Davis in the league (unless current San Francisco 49'er Anthony Davis retires from the NFL and takes his svelte 6'5", 323 lb. frame to the NBA to sign with the Milwaukee Bucks who play in his favorite state of Wisconsin) and you cannot see Randle having all that much trouble scoring against the likes of most NBA starting power forwards, including defensive dynamo's such as Jared Sullinger, Ersan Ilyasova, Josh McRoberts and Carlos Boozer, or even superstar power forwards such as Kevin Love and Dirk Nowitzki. Simply put, Julius Randle looks like exactly what a future great NBA power forward should look like at a young 19 years of age

Doug McDermott: This 6'8, 223 lb., 22 year old combo forward and coach's son has perhaps the most complete and varied offensive game of any player in the draft if not the most dynamic and explosive. The kid known as *Dougie McBuckets* can score as easily in the post as he can from the perimeter and is incredibly efficient from, well, everywhere.

One major knock on McDermott is his age as he will turn 23 years old during his rookie season and therefore some seem to feel he doesn't have as much potential as other small forwards in this draft such as Croatian Dario Saric or even Syracuse sophomore wingman Jerami Grant. The other and frankly more worrisome concern with McDermott is his lack of lateral quickness and ability to guard NBA level small forwards. If you thought watching Nick Young or Ryan Kelly get burned on back door cuts and drives to the bucket was painful, imagine what someone without half of Nick Young's athleticism or even close to Ryan Kelly's length will give up on the defensive end.

Some seem to believe McDermott's ceiling could be an NBA great such as Bernard King while his floor could be a player such as Wally Szczerbiak, albeit with a better attitude and post-game. And, while Szczerbiak's name may not make one think of greatness, remember that Wally had a solid 10 year career in the league, thrice averaged over 17 points per game for an entire season, made the All-Star team and was in fact one of the best pure shooters and most efficient wing scorers in league history. That's not a bad floor all things considered.

However, will Celtics fans really be happy with you spending the sixth pick in the deepest draft since 1996 on a rich man's Wally Szczerbiak? Then again, does it matter what Celtics fans will think if such a player gives you the best opportunity to win a ring this year?

Have you decided who you will select? Are you confident in your decision? Well, before you head up to that podium to hand in your pick you might want to see who in the world would be calling you right now and pick up your ringing phone.

Phoenix Suns General Manager Ryan McDonough: *Hello, this is Ryan McDonough. I know you're about to make your pick. However, I also know you're trying to dump Gerald Wallace's nasty contract and haven't found any takers. Well listen, I've got an offer for you but this offer isn't open for negotiation. You can either take it or leave it.*

Utah Jazz GM Dennis Lindsey is already on board with this deal. I had to give up my Matt Stone and Trey Parker autographed 'The Book of Mormon' playbill but it's all good, Lindsey's on board and if you agree we can get this deal done fast.

You will receive Goran Dragic, Gordon Hayward (in a Sign and Trade that will see him receive a four year, forty-million deal, with a starting salary of $9,367,682 and 4.5 percent annual raises) and Channing Frye in exchange for Rajon Rondo and Gerald Wallace. We will be sending our rights to the Wizards and Pacers first round picks we own this year to the Jazz while acquiring Rondo, and the Jazz will be the ones taking back Gerald Wallace's nasty contract in exchange for the rights to the Wizards and Pacers picks.

Basically you're trading Rondo for Dragic, Frye and two first-rounders and then re-directing those two first-rounders along with Gerald Wallace to the Jazz for Gordon Hayward.

That's my offer and I'm not waiting more than five seconds for your answer.
So, what's your answer? Do we have a deal or not?

If you agree to trade Rondo and Wallace for Hayward, Dragic and Frye,
turn to page 47.

If you decline McDonough's trade offer,
turn to page 48.

Celtics CEO Wyc Grousbeck: *Whoa! You traded Rondo? You definitely aren't wasting any time making your mark on this team I guess.*

I don't really know what to say. Part of me wants to slap your face, kick you in the stomach and fire you on the spot. However, part of me is excited with the prospects of reuniting Gordon Hayward with Coach Stevens and letting Goran Dragic run this team. Channing Frye's not a bad throw-in either if I do say so myself.

I spoke with my Danny Ainge and asked him what he thought about this. He told me he wouldn't have traded Rondo but that he can't say you got jipped in this deal either. He actually was pretty impressed you got such a great package for Rondo and especially that you were able to dump Gerald Wallace's horrendous contract. I saw his point and the more I thought about it and continue to think about it, this trade may actually have been ingenious.

I'm going to give you the benefit of the doubt here and see how this plays out. Watch yourself though and don't think for one second that I won't fire you on the spot if you execute an idiotic trade, because I will!

Continue on to page 49.

Celtics CEO Wyc Grousbeck: *You were offered Goran Dragic and Gordon Hayward and the expiring contract of Channing Frye and the ability to dump Gerald Wallace's nasty contract for Rajon Rondo and you turned it down? Are you kidding me?*

One of the reasons I decided Danny Ainge wasn't capable of running the entire show is due to his failure to trade Rondo already and also due to his accepting Gerald Wallace's contract in the Garnett and Pierce deal last season. I hired you because I thought you had the guts to make the tough decisions, to put the team ahead of any individual player and to build me a title winning roster. I was wrong.

You had the opportunity to change this team, to really build a champion. That power was in your hands and you refused to do anything with it. You're fired!

**You're journey has ended.
Enjoy being an armchair GM.**

Words of Wisdom:

At the end of the day, you're responsible for yourself and your actions and that's all you can control. So rather than be frustrated with what you can't control, try to fix the things you can.

- Kevin Garnett

After agreeing to trade Rajon Rondo and Gerald Wallace for Goran Dragic, Gordon Hayward and Channing Frye you realize you need to decide who you are going to draft immediately, and decide to:

**Draft Dante Exum. If this is your choice,
turn to page 50.**

**Draft Julius Randle. If this is your choice,
turn to page 51.**

**Draft Doug McDermott. If this is your choice,
turn to page 52.**

Celtics CEO Wyc Grousbeck: *Dante Exum had a solid rookie season. In fact, it wouldn't shock me if this kid becomes the best player out of this entire draft when all is said and done.*

However, the kid just wasn't ready to play quality minutes on a championship level team as a rookie. Plus, the poor kid can't shoot! I mean come on, .398 from the field and .225 from deep; that's horrible! The fans might love the kid but what good is that when you can't shoot to save your own life? A team can't win without making shots!

We might have won 49 games and snagged the fifth seed in the East but the Brooklyn Nets kicked out butt in the first round and that makes me sick! You shouldn't have drafted Exum, not when you knew you had to win a title immediately. You're fired!

You're journey has ended.
Enjoy being an armchair GM.

Words of Wisdom:

I got by on talent. That was my fatal mistake.

- Pete Maravich

Celtics CEO Wyc Grousbeck: *It's beast time baby! Julius Randle is a beast; great pick!*

I was worried you were going to draft Dante Exum or even Doug McDermott. I mean, don't get me wrong, Exum could be an amazing player one day but the kid can't shoot and he's just too young and inexperienced to count on at this stage of his career. As for McDermott, if there's one thing that kid can do it's shoot, but he can't defend and in today's NBA you've got to be able to defend.

Anyways, I am thrilled with this pick and think you just drafted a future superstar. Again, great work!

Continue on to page 53.

Celtics CEO Wyc Grousbeck: *Doug McDermott's rookie year can be summed up in one word: steady. The kid averaged 16.1 points per game while shooting .492 from the field and .408 from distance which is pretty awesome. In fact the kid even looks as if he could easily play a decade in this league and go down as one of the most efficient scorers in NBA history.*

However, Dougie McBuckets also had the reputation of being a bit of a black hole on the offensive end and gave up a whole lot of McBuckets on the defensive end too. It was as if the kid thought he was still playing for his dad at Creighton and all he had to do was score.

We might have won 45 games and earned the seventh seed in the Eastern Conference but we got slaughtered by the Pacers in the first round and you didn't get the job done. You're fired!

You're journey has ended.
Enjoy being an armchair GM.

Words of Wisdom:

It's hard when your father's the coach. Sometimes you don't know where one leaves off and the other begins.

- Pete Maravich

After drafting Julius Randle you watched the draft unfold much as you thought it would. There weren't any shocking picks such as Anthony Bennett to the Cavaliers with the number one overall pick in last year's draft.

When it came time for you to make your second selection, a pick that originally belonged to the Brooklyn Nets, there were once again three more players you had sincere interest in.

Shabazz Napier: This 6'1, 182 lb., soon to be 23 year old point guard is coming off his second NCAA championship and a dominant NCAA Tournament run in which he was voted the *Most Outstanding Player* of the *Final Four*. Napier is known as a gamer, for being clutch and for having the mysterious *it*.

Napier is a very good scorer who can get his own shot whenever he wants it and also scores efficiently as noted by his .405 three-point average and .870 free-throw average. He is also a fantastic rebounder for his size (6.7 rebounds per 40 minutes), very good passer (5.6 assists per 40 minutes) and incredibly plucky defender who seems to annoy opposing point guards each and every game he plays in.

Perhaps the only real knocks on Napier's game are that he may not have much room to improve due to his advanced age and that he does not possess elite athleticism. However, even if Napier has hit his ceiling, he is already starting point guard quality. And, while he does not have elite athleticism that does not seem to affect his on-court performances even when matched up against elite defenders like Florida's Scottie Wilbekin or much larger and stronger defenders like Kentucky's Aaron Harrison. Simply put, while Napier may be a reach this early in the draft based on his potential, or lack thereof, he may also be just about the safest pick in the draft as well.

Kyle Anderson: This 6'8, 233 lb., 20 year old jack-of-all-trades from UCLA is an extremely intriguing player and has been called a poor man's Magic Johnson. His per game averages of 14.6 points, 8.8 rebounds and 6.5 assists in just 33.2 minutes per game attest to the Magic comparisons. Anderson projects to playing small forward in the NBA but has magnificent point guard skills and is a prototypical point-forward if ever there was one.

Anderson has an amazing feel for the game and is one of the best ball handlers in the entire draft. He also has an insane 7'2.5" wingspan and 9' standing reach which of course could present a myriad of problems for opponents, especially if Anderson happens to be playing guard at the time.

Anderson does have his detractors however and there are some serious concerns with how his game will translate to the NBA level. He has below average athleticism and an awkward looking jump-shot that he is not very consistent with whatsoever. However, he does seem to be able to get his shot off when he wants thanks to an array of old-man-moves. He also is a fantastic rebounder despite his limited athleticism and while his jump shot is anything but pretty he does shoot very respectable percentages from inside the arc, long-range and the free-throw line. All things considered, Anderson is an extremely intriguing prospect and could turn out to be one of the longest lasting NBA players in this draft and a player who makes an All-Star game or three as well, before all is said and done.

Adreian Payne: This 6'9", 215 lb., 23 year old power forward with the varied offensive game reminds you of a better shooting Terrence Jones of the Houston Rockets, albeit with less upside so to speak. Payne had a solid career at Michigan State and thanks to Tom Izzo's coaching, is certainly ready to be an instant contributor to a playoff level squad.

Payne is known not only for his monster dunks but for his three-point proficiency as well. He also averaged a very impressive 16.4 points and 7.3 rebounds (as well as 23.3 points and 10.4 rebounds per 40 minutes) during his senior season, in which he also shot .536 from the floor and an incredible .423 from deep. Payne is also knows as a great teammate and high-character individual. He famously befriended Lacey *Princess* Holsworth, a precious little six year old girl who was suffering from a rare form of nerve cancer. Payne and Holsworth remained close friends until her passing (may she rest in peace and in the presence of the Lord) shortly after the 2014 NCAA season ended and she and her family referred to Payne as superman.

The only real concern with Payne is that he doesn't have a normal lung capacity. Simply put, he has a hard time getting enough air and can therefore get tired out faster than he normally would if he had normal lung capacity. This said, it's very possible he will never be able to play a solid 36 minutes night in and night out over the course of an NBA season.

You are now on the clock. Do you want to:

**Draft Shabazz Napier. If this is your choice,
turn to page 57.**

**Draft Kyle Anderson. If this is your choice,
turn to page 58.**

**Draft Adreian Payne. If this is your choice,
turn to page 59.**

Celtics CEO Wyc Grousbeck: *Shabazz Napier had a very good rookie season. In fact he would have been a great pick … had you picked him in the late first round or early second round where he was projected to be picked. However, you reached and it cost you.*

Shabazz shot the ball fine and even defended pretty well. However, he was turnover prone and that hurt us, especially when Goran Dragic went down in the first round of the playoffs with an ankle injury. Napier just couldn't be trusted not to turn the ball over and seemed to be more interested in making a flashy play than the correct play.

I don't think he was consciously trying to be a hot-dog. I actually think he just thinks so highly of his own abilities that he believes he can pull off insane passes that he just can't. Regardless, his turnovers hurt us.

We won 52 games and snagged the fourth seed in the East but the Brooklyn Nets knocked us out in six games in the first round. I didn't hire you to win two playoff games. You're fired!

You're journey has ended.
Enjoy being an armchair GM.

Words of Wisdom:

They don't pay you a million dollars for two-hand chest passes.

- Pete Maravich

Celtics CEO Wyc Grousbeck: *Nice pick! I'm very excited to see this Kyle 'baby-Magic' Anderson kid play. I don't know a whole lot about him but from the little tape I've watched and from all Danny Ainge told me about him, I am really excited he's a Celtic.*

I was afraid you were going to draft Shabazz Napier just because he led the Connecticut Huskies to the NCAA Title last season. I remember some fans back in 2000 hoping the Celtics would draft Mateen Cleaves after he led the Michigan State Spartans to the NCAA Title. I knew he wasn't going to be any good in the NBA but many of my friends thought he would be the next great point guard. Of course the Celtics didn't draft Mateen, though they didn't do any better drafting Jerome Moiso. Regardless that 2000 Draft was maybe the worst in history, it was just brutal. But, you get the point. Just because someone is great in college doesn't mean they're going to be great in the NBA.

However, this Kyle Anderson kid looks like he could be the real deal. You smart to swing for the fences and take a risk with this pick. Great job; keep up the good work!

Continue on to page 61.

Celtics CEO Wyc Grousbeck: *Adreian Payne was a decent pick. However, I didn't hire you to do a decent job, I hired you to win a title immediately. That didn't happen.*

Payne put up some great per-40 numbers with 20 points and 10 rebounds. However, those numbers don't mean a whole lot when you consider that Payne only played 19 minutes a game and seemed to be constantly gasping for air and needing a rest on the bench after just four to six minutes of on-court action.

We did win 51 games and earn the fourth seed in the East which was decent. However, the Brooklyn Nets knocked us out in the first round, and, again, I didn't hire you to a 'decent' job; I hired you to win me a title immediately!

You failed to win a title. You're fired. Now, get out of my office!

You're journey has ended.
Enjoy being an armchair GM.

Words of Wisdom:

I don't think anything less than perfect, even though I'm a human being. The way I work and go at things is to better myself in perfect terms.

- Kevin Garnett

RE-SIGNING YOUR OWN FREE AGENTS

After trading Rajon Rondo and Gerald Wallace for Goran Dragic, Gordon Hayward and Channing Frye, and drafting Julius Randle and Kyle Anderson, your roster currently looks as follows, complete with each player's 2014-15 salary:

Starting Point Guard:	Goran Dragic	$7,500,000
Starting Shooting Guard:	Gordon Hayward	$9,367,682
Starting Small Forward:	Jeff Green	$9,200,000
Starting Power Forward:	Julius Randle	$3,283,320
Starting Center:	Kelly Olynyk	$2,075,760
Backup Point Guard:	Empty Roster Spot	
Backup Shooting Guard:	Empty Roster Spot	
Backup Small Forward:	Kyle Anderson	$1,674,480
Backup Power Forward:	Jared Sullinger	$1,424,520
Backup Center:	Channing Frye	$6,800,000
Reserve Point Guard:	Empty Roster Spot	
Reserve Shooting Guard:	Empty Roster Spot	
Reserve Small Forward:	Empty Roster Spot	
Reserve Power Forward:	Brandon Bass	$6,950,000
Reserve Center:	Joel Anthony	$3,800,000

Furthermore, after signing Julius Randle to a contract that will pay him $3,283,320 this season and Kyle Anderson to a contract that will pay him $1,674,480 this season, you have exactly $52,075,762 on the books. With the salary cap set at $63,200,000 this season and the luxury tax threshold being set at $77,000,000 you have exactly $11,124,238 to spend on a minimum of two free agents.

Also, understand that under league rules you are allowed to exceed the salary cap to sign players to minimum contracts as long as you figure in a cap hold of $507,336 for each player under the 12 man limit that remains unsigned, and you do not exceed the luxury tax threshold. For example let's pretend that the Oklahoma City Thunder trio of Kevin Durant, Russell Westbrook and Serge Ibaka were all free agents this year and that each demanded and could be paid $19,544,658. A team with an empty roster could literally sign all three players to such maximum contracts as doing so would give that team a total salary of $58,633,974 and leave the team with $4,566,026 in remaining cap space as well as nine player spots to fill, and it just so happens that $4,556,026 divided nine ways works out to the NBA minimum salary of exactly $507,336, with an ole two dollar bill to spare.

The above said, if such a situation occurred and a team signed Durant, Westbrook and Ibaka, that team would not be barred from spending more than an additional $4,556,026 on the remaining nine or more players if such occurred in merely offering minimum contracts. Such a team would simply be barred from signing any one player to anything more than a minimum contract. However, as veterans who have played ten plus seasons in the league receive a minimum salary of $1,448,490 rather than the NBA minimum of $507,336, it is possible that the team that signed Durant, Westbrook and Ibaka to contracts totaling $58,633,974 could still sign twelve such 10-plus-season-veterans to contracts totaling another $17,381,880. If a team were to do this, they would have an actual team salary of $76,015,854, even though the salary cap is just $63,200,000 this season, as they did not exceed the luxury tax threshold of $77,000,000.

All of above said, you need to be careful that you do not sign players in early free agency to standard contracts if you feel such players could be added later on minimum contracts, as to do so would be to reduce your available cap space and possibly sabotage your ability to build a title-contending roster. Simply put, you need to spend wisely or else!

The first thing you will need to do is decide which, if any, players from last year's disappointing squad you would like to re-sign, as all of them are willing to re-sign for the right price. That said it's now time to go through the list and see the contractual demands of ach player from last year's roster which you can then either accept or decline. If you accept a player's demands that player will be wearing green and white next season; if you decline to accept a player's demands that player will sign elsewhere.

Would you like to re-sign Jerryd Bayless to a four year $22,000,000 contract that will pay him $5,500,000 in each season, Vitor Faverani to a four year $12,000,000 contract that will pay him $3,000,000 in each season?

If your answer is no, turn to page 65.

If your answer is yes, turn to page 66.

Celtics CEO Wyc Grousbeck: *Thank you for not re-signing Jerryd Bayless and Vitor Faverani. Both players are young and talented and could make a name for themselves in this league one day, but I would have slapped you silly and fired you on the spot had you paid them the sort of loot they were asking for.*

There is just no way they were worth the figures they were demanding. You were wise to let them walk and hold onto your cap space. Great job! Now, get out there and sign me a couple of quality players.

Continue on to page 67.

Celtics CEO Wyc Grousbeck: *Re-signing Jerryd Bayless and Vitor Faverani wasn't a horrible decision talent wise, but signing them to contracts that paid them a total of eight-and-a-half million this season was insane! You could have spent that loot on another player or players that would have contributed much more to the team's success this season than Jerryd and Vitor did.*

I feel like you just sort of slacked off and chose the easy path, rather than actually working and giving your all to this job. You didn't even try to negotiate them down on their wild demands and just gave in immediately. I don't feel like you gave 100%, not even close, and that disgusts me.

We won 45 games and earned the sixth seed and all. However, no sooner had we made the playoffs than the Chicago Bulls swept us right out of them. I can't stand the Bulls and I can't stand losing! You're fired!

You're journey has ended.
Enjoy being an armchair GM.

Words of Wisdom:

I've got a theory that if you give 100% all of the time, somehow things will work out in the end.

- Larry Bird

Would you like to exercise your one-year $915,000 team options on Christapher Johnson and Chris Babb as well as re-sign Phil Pressey to a one year $915,000 contract as well? Or, would you rather save the $2,745,000 to spend on another free agent and possibly re-sign these three young players to minimum contracts at a later date?

If you would like to sign Johnson, Pressey and Babb, turn to page 68.

If you would like to decline your team options on Johnson and Babb as well as decline to sign Phil Pressey at this time, turn to page 69.

Celtics CEO Wyc Grousbeck: *I'm furious, just furious! You knew full well that our cap space was running low and yet you signed three young no-name players that you could almost undoubtedly sign to minimum contracts at a later date?*

Don't you know anything about financial prudence, disciplined investing, hedging your bets and making wise decisions? You should have learned from history, through the mistakes of former General Managers like Isaih Thomas and Otis Smith who made horrible financial decisions which cost them their jobs. But, you didn't learn from history, you laughed in the face of it and went out and spent a bunch of our cap space on minimum level players.

You're fired! Go take some business courses at your local junior college as you have no chance of getting a GM gig anytime soon.

You're journey has ended.
Enjoy being an armchair GM.

Words of Wisdom:

I don't think you should ever run from history. You should learn from it and embrace it.

- Doc Rivers

Celtics CEO Wyc Grousbeck: *Good decision. Danny Ainge and I really like Christapher, Phil and Chris as players and would love to see all of them on the team next year, but to give up much needed cap space to sign them right now makes no sense at all.*

Nice job. Keep up the good work and sign me a quality player or two!

Continue on to page 70.

Would you like to re-sign Kris Humphries to a four year $28,000,000 deal that will pay him $7,000,000 each season and Keith Bogans to a three year $6,000,000 contract that will pay him $2,000,000 each season?

If your answer is yes, turn to page 71.

If your answer is no, turn to page 72.

Celtics CEO Wyc Grousbeck: *You gave Kris Humphries and Keith Bogans a combined thirty-four million dollars and used just about all of the cap space you had left on them? That is the dumbest, most asinine, shockingly stupid thing I have ever heard of.*

You make Isaih Thomas look like a disciplined investor; there is just no way I can trust you anymore. I don't care if I just hired you, you're fired. Get out of my office and never show your face around here again; never!

You're journey has ended.
Enjoy being an armchair GM.

Words of Wisdom:

I accomplished what I set out to do, but I lost my discipline and my career.

- Pete Maravich

Celtics CEO Wyc Grousbeck: *Duh. That was the easiest choice you may ever have to make in life. Deciding whether or not to pay Kris Humphries and Keith Bogans a combined thirty-four million dollars is easier than deciding whether or not to stare at the sun until your eyes fry out of your head.*

Had you agreed to Humphries and Bogans' ridiculous contract demands I would have fired you on the spot. So, um, congratulations on not being an idiot.

Continue on to page 73.

Would you like to re-sign Avery Bradley to a five year $30,000,000 contract with 7.5 percent annual raises that will see him earn $5,217,391 this season?

If your answer is yes, turn to page 74.

If your answer is no, turn to page 75.

Celtics CEO Wyc Grousbeck: *Great signing! I am really beginning to trust your judgment and think I hired a future 'Executive of the Year'.*

Avery Bradley has improved every year he's been in the league and the kid's defense alone is worth millions per year. Had you failed to re-sign Avery I would have been mad. Had you failed to re-sign him at the low price of twenty-five mil over 5 years I would have been madder than Alex Rodriguez at an arbitration hearing!

Great job! Keep up the good work!
Continue on to page 77.

Celtics CEO Wyc Grousbeck: *You didn't agree to pay Avery Bradley a mere six-mil per year? Come on man, what's wrong with you? Avery is one of the best defensive combo-guards on the planet and the kid is getting better every year as an offensive player as well.*

I'm disgusted. I'm just sick to my stomach over your failure to sign one of the best young players we have had in years. Danny Ainge feels you have done a good enough job so far to keep your position but honestly I don't really care what Danny thinks this time. I loved Avery and believe that your failure to re-sign him is a fire-able offence.

You're fired. Did I stutter? I said you're fired; now, get out of my office!

You're journey has ended.
Enjoy being an armchair GM.

Words of Wisdom:

Concentration and mental toughness are the margins of victory.

- Bill Russell

SIGNING THE LEAGUE'S FREE AGENTS

After re-signing Avery Bradley, your roster currently looks as follows, complete with each player's 2014-15 salary:

Starting Point Guard:	Goran Dragic	$7,500,000
Starting Shooting Guard:	Gordon Hayward	$9,367,682
Starting Small Forward:	Jeff Green	$9,200,000
Starting Power Forward:	Julius Randle	$3,283,320
Starting Center:	Kelly Olynyk	$2,075,760
Backup Point Guard:	Empty Roster Spot	
Backup Shooting Guard:	Avery Bradley	$5,217,391
Backup Small Forward:	Kyle Anderson	$1,674,480
Backup Power Forward:	Jared Sullinger	$1,424,520
Backup Center:	Channing Frye	$6,800,000
Reserve Point Guard:	Empty Roster Spot	
Reserve Shooting Guard:	Empty Roster Spot	
Reserve Small Forward:	Empty Roster Spot	
Reserve Power Forward:	Brandon Bass	$6,950,000
Reserve Center:	Joel Anthony	$3,800,000

You now have 11 players and exactly $57,293,153 on the books. You also now have just $5,906,847 in cap space, all of which you can offer to just one free agent.

You realize that your most pressing need is a backup point guard and set your sights on signing the best available free agent point guard you can get your hands on. However, there are just two such players who's agents have informed you they will sign for an amount you can afford. They are as follows:

Mario Chalmers: This 28 year old point guard is known for being a winner, period. With multiple NBA rings and an NCAA Title to boot, in which he hit a dagger-three over superstar Derrick Rose to help lead the Kansas Jayhawks over Rose's Memphis Tigers.

Chalmers is more of a scoring point guard than a true floor-general. However, while he is certainly not a dynamic, let alone dominant, scorer, he is one of the most efficient scoring point guards in the league today, as evidenced by his incredibly high effective field goal percentage.

The primary concerns with Chalmers are twofold. Firstly, that he is not a dynamic athlete yet would rather score than pass. And secondly, that he seems to enjoy playing hero-ball and desires to be the man, or at least one of the top three options on a team, after spending the past four years in the shadow of LeBron James, Dwyane Wade and Chris Bosh on the Miami Heat.

Greivis Vasquez: This 27 year old combo guard is known for being an incredibly feisty competitor as well as for leading the entire NBA in assists during the 2012-13 season.

Vasquez is a true floor general and pass-first point guard who can also score at a pretty solid clip, even if he is only an average shooter. He was considered one of the most promising young point guards in the game just two short years ago before he was traded to the Sacramento Kings and later the Toronto Raptors and his minutes decreased dramatically. However, in Toronto he helped solidify the Raptors bench and lead the team to its first playoff appearance in six seasons.

The primary concern with Vasquez is his lack of foot speed, though honestly he may not be all that much slower than Mario Chalmers. Vasquez is a below average defender due to this lack of foot speed, though having him guard the opposing team's shooting guard can mask some of his weaknesses.

Mario Chalmers agents has made it clear that his client will accept a four year, $24,000,000 contract with 4.5 percent annual raises and a starting salary of $5,620,609 while Greivis Vasquez's agent has stated that his client will accept a one-year, $5,750,000 contract in the hopes that he can parlay such a deal into a much more lucrative contract the following year.

If you would like to sign Chalmers,
turn to page 80.

If you would like to sign Vasquez,
turn to page 81.

If you decline to offer either Mario Chalmers or
Greivis Vasquez a contract,
turn to page 82.

Celtics CEO Wyc Grousbeck: *I was really excited when you signed Mario Chalmers. How can you go wrong signing a multi-time NBA champion and one-time NCAA champion who's known for hitting clutch shots?*

However, while Mario was certainly one of the best backup point guards in the league this season, he actually seemed to take serious umbrage with the fact that he wasn't starting over Goran Dragic. He could have thrived in his role and won '6th Man of the Year' but be made the worst it instead.

With Chalmers providing solid minutes at the back-up point guard spot, we managed to win 54 games and nab the fourth seed in the East. When we knocked out the Brooklyn Nets in the first round, I was on cloud nine and dreaming of a title. However, as soon as the first game of our second round match-up against LeBron James and the Cleveland Cavaliers ended with us getting thumped 121-79 I realized the dream was never going to become a reality. It didn't as the Cavs swept us out of the playoffs and now you're fired!

You're journey has ended.
Enjoy being an armchair GM.

Words of Wisdom:

I learned one thing – never hate a positive option.

- Kevin Garnett

Celtics CEO Wyc Grousbeck: *Greivis Vasquez hmm? I'm not so sure that was the right choice. Personally I would have rather you signed Mario Chalmers but I do trust you. Wow, did I really just say that? In all seriousness, you have done a great job so far and I really like the roster you've put together. So, while I personally would have signed Chalmers over Vasquez, I will give you the benefit of the doubt and patiently wait to see how things play out.*

You've got a solid 12 man roster right now. Just go snap up three minimum contract players, preferably Christapher Johnson, Phil Pressey and Chris Babb if they will accept minimum deals, and let's get this show on the road and start winning games!

Continue on to page 83.

Celtics CEO Wyc Grousbeck: *I can't believe you didn't sign anyone with the remaining cap space you had to play with? What in the world were you planning to do with the extra loot, pocket it and escape to Costa Rica like 'Ivan Block' in 'Runner Runner'?*

I told you that you would have to win a title this year or that you'd be fired. Then you go out and refuse to spend the cap space we had? Did you think you were playing Moneyball with Billy Bean? Crazy! I don't even know what to say at this point. I know you were scared that Chalmers and Vasquez both could hurt team chemistry but you had to take a chance on one of them, you just had too!

We now have no good options left at the back-up point guard and I have lost all faith in you. You're fired, effective immediately; now get out!

You're journey has ended.
Enjoy being an armchair GM.

Words of Wisdom:

As a coach, you've got to do what's best for the team. If guys don't like it, they're going to leave. If they stay and don't like it, well, your team's going to suck anyway. Even if this happens, you still have to do it. You can't coach worrying about any individual.

- Doc Rivers

After signing Greivis Vasquez to be your Celtics back-up point guard, you now have just three roster spots left to fill and all you need is a third-string point guard, shooting guard and small forward. However, you have only minimum contracts to offer as you have just $156,847 remaining in cap space.

There are three interesting options at your disposal to fill your teams need for a third-string point guard, shooting guard and small forward.

The first option is to bring back three of last season's Celtics: Christapher Johnson, Phil Pressey and Chris Babby.

All three of the above players would provide youth and athleticism off the bench as well as potential. You would also know what you're getting as all three have played for the Celtics and none are known to be high-maintenance individuals.

The second option is to sign three former all-stars: Stephon Marbury, Chauncey Billups and Tracy McGrady.

All three of the above players have big names, no doubt about that. McGrady is a former multi-time scoring champ, Marbury was known as *Starbury* during his heyday and Billups is known as *Mr. Big Shot* and has an *NBA Finals MVP* trophy on his resume. However, only Billups played in the league last year and he had anything but a solid season. Signing these three players is a classic high-risk high-reward dilemma.

The third option is to sign three of the best street-ballers on the planet today: Patrick Robinson aka *Pat the Roc*, Hugh Jones aka *Baby Shaq* and Anthony Pimble aka *Mr. Afrika*.

All three of the above players would bring an incredible amount of energy and athleticism to the team, not to mention entertainment and everyone knows fans love to be entertained. Robinson played for the Cincinnati Bearcats when he was 5'9" and amazingly grew to 6'2" after leaving college and his game has grown with him. Pimble won back-to-back conference titles at Ventura Community College in California and is known for his insane dunking ability.

And Jones is perhaps the best known player and someone many, including Shaquille O'Neal, think should have been in the NBA years ago. You can learn more about these players at the **www.ballup.com** website.

If you would like to sign Johnson, Pressey and Babb, turn to page 85.

If you would like to sign Marbury, Billups and McGrady, turn to page 86.

If you would like to sign Robinson, Jones and Pimble, turn to page 87.

Celtics CEO Wyc Grousbeck: *Thank you for taking my hint that Danny Ainge and I wanted to see Christapher, Phil and Chris back in the green and white. I really appreciate that and once again you have given me a reason to trust you. Nice work.*

Now, our entire 15 man roster is set and I am geeked. I can't wait for the season to get started. However, don't get cocky and don't even think about getting complacent. We have no idea how this season is going to play out and you may have to work some of your own trade magic before the trade deadline passes.

For now though, go and celebrate, you've built a great roster and made me very happy. Great job!

Continue onto page 89.

Celtics CEO Wyc Grousbeck: *Signing former All-Stars Stephon Marbury, Chauncey Billups and Tracy McGrady was a risky move. Every single one of them played solid offensive basketball individually and put up decent per minute stats but chemistry was always an issue and defense was an even bigger issue and both ended up costing us big-time.*

We got off to a rough start going 10-8 to start the season but finished on a high note winning 55 games and earning the fourth seed in the Western Conference. We even knocked off the Brooklyn Nets in the first round. However, in the second round we ran into LeBron James' Cavaliers and then they ran us out of the gym. The former all-stars you signed couldn't keep up with Cleveland's young legs and were just torched defensively. It was a disaster.

I didn't hire you to witness a disaster. You're fired!

You're journey has ended.
Enjoy being an armchair GM.

Words of Wisdom:

Basketball is like war in that offensive weapons are developed first, and it always takes a while for the defense to catch up.

- Red Aeurbach

Celtics CEO Wyc Grousbeck: *Who would have guessed that signing four street ballers would turn out to be a bad decision? Um, only every NBA executive on the planet other than you!*

I know the fans were clamoring for you to sign the guys from the Ball Up squad as fans love to see sick dunks and crazy passes and all that but you can't take instructions from the fans. Many of them never even played organized basketball!

It's also not as if the guys you signed were Joe 'the Destroyer' Hammond, Earl 'the Goat' Manigault, Rick 'Pee Wee' Kirkland and Ed 'Booger' Smith. Had you signed those guys in their primes you wouldn't be in my office right now, you'd be at a championship parade. But you didn't sign those guys did you? No!

We may have snuck into the playoffs as a seventh seed but we were also the laughing stock of the league this year and led the NBA in turnovers! Getting swept by the Pacers in the first round was the final nail in your coffin. You're fired!

You're journey has ended.
Enjoy being an armchair GM.

Words of Wisdom:

Shooting is nothing. Anybody can shoot. The big charge is putting on a show for the crowd.

- Pete Maravich

CELTICS 2014-I5 ROSTER

After filling your final roster spot by signing Greivis Vasquez, Christapher Johnson, Phil Pressey and Chris Babb your Boston Celtics 2014-15 roster is set and looks as follows:

Starting Point Guard:	Goran Dragic	$7,500,000
Starting Shooting Guard:	Gordon Hayward	$9,367,682
Starting Small Forward:	Jeff Green	$9,200,000
Starting Power Forward:	Julius Randle	$3,283,320
Starting Center:	Kelly Olynyk	$2,075,760
Backup Point Guard:	Greivis Vasquez	$5,750,000
Backup Shooting Guard:	Avery Bradley	$5,217,391
Backup Small Forward:	Kyle Anderson	$1,674,480
Backup Power Forward:	Jared Sullinger	$1,424,520
Backup Center:	Channing Frye	$6,800,000
Reserve Point Guard:	Phil Pressey	$816,482
Reserve Shooting Guard:	Chris Babb	$816,482
Reserve Small Forward:	Christa. Johnson	$915,243
Reserve Power Forward:	Brandon Bass	$6,950,000
Reserve Center:	Joel Anthony	$3,800,000

With the roster set, team salary set at $65,591,360 and training camp about to start in less than six weeks, it's now time to sit back and enjoy watching the team you built destroy the competition. However, again, don't get cocky or complacent as you may need to work some trade magic at some point this season.

THE MID-WAY POINT

At the mid-way point of the season and thanks in large part to the best bench in the NBA by far, your Celtics sit firmly atop the Atlantic Division with a 26-15 record. If the playoffs were to start today they would be the East's number four seed, behind only the LeBron James and Kyrie Irving led Cleveland Cavaliers, Indiana Pacers and Chicago Bulls. A second round Playoff appearance seems like a foregone conclusion if the team can stay healthy, yet a Conference title, let alone an NBA championship may still be an extreme long-shot, thanks to *King James* and his dominant Cavaliers squad.

Over in the Western Conference, the Thunder and superstars Kevin Durant and Russell Westbrook have been steamrolling the competition. The Thunder have a full four game lead on the Houston Rockets for the best record in the East and sit just a half game behind the Cleveland Cavaliers for the best record in the NBA.

It was shocking news when LeBron James decided to opt out of the final year of his contract with the Miami Heat and re-join the team that drafted him, especially after Cavs owner Dan Gilbert went all *Adolf* and publicly denounced James for leaving. However, the man known as *King James* was never stupid. He showed his basketball intelligence when he signed with the Heat and then went out and won multiple titles, and he showed it again this past summer when he left the aging Heat to sign with a Cavs team loaded with young talent and another legit superstar with his best days ahead of him in Kyrie Irving. And now, LeBron is once again reaping the rewards of his prudent basketball decision-making.

While your Celtics seem to be rolling in the East, or at least in their own Atlantic Division, you may need to make a trade or two to assure yourself a title this season, as as-is the team has the look of little more than an Eastern Conference Finals stepping stone for the Cavaliers to win their first franchise title. That said, don't be afraid to rock the boat if need be as your future as Celtics GM may depend on you doing so.

If the playoffs were to begin today each Conference's top eight seeds would look as follows:

Eastern Conference

1. Cleveland Cavaliers

2. Indiana Pacers

3. Chicago Bulls

4. Boston Celtics

5. Brooklyn Nets

6. Toronto Raptors

7. Charlotte Bobcats

8. Miami Heat

Western Conference

1. Oklahoma City Thunder

2. Houston Rockets

3. Los Angeles Clippers

4. San Antonio Spurs

5. Golden State Warriors

6. Portland Trailblazers

7. Dallas Mavericks

8. Minnesota Timberwolves

Several Celtics are embedded in the various individual trophy races as well. Brad Stevens seems like a shoe-in to win *Coach of the Year* though Cleveland's John Calipari – who LeBron James lured away from Kentucky – is likely a strong second, even if LeBron James is the real coach of that Cavaliers squad. Jared Sullinger also looks like the front-runner to win the *6th Man of the Year* award, thanks in large part to his 15.0 points and 9.1 rebounds per game and the fact that voters don't seem to mind if a player couldn't guard their mother on the defensive end (see Steve Nash's two MVP trophies for proof of this sad fact) when they're voting. And, Kelly Olynyk seems to be in a two-man race with fellow sophomore Anthony Bennett for the *Most Improved Player* award, thanks to his solid all-around contributions as your starting center and averaging in 13.4 points, 8.7 rebound and 2.6 assists in 30.5 minutes per game.

Julius Randle also seems to be leading the pack in the race for the *Rookie of the Year* award, though Andrew Wiggins and Marcus Smart aren't far behind. However, seeing as Randle is fourth amongst rookies in scoring and averaging more rebounds than any other rookie by far with 9.6 per game, and especially seeing as Randle will most likely be the only top rookie to make the playoffs, he may just be a lock to win *R.O.Y.* ... unless of course Kyle Anderson keeps up his recent torrid pace!

Kyle Anderson has been a very, very pleasant surprise for your Celtics this year, and while his first 20 games or so didn't go all that well, his last 10 games have been amazing. With Avery Bradley missing the last two weeks with an ankle sprain, Anderson has received the bulk of the bench minutes at the backup one, two and three spots, and has responded by playing his best ball of the season. In the last 10 games Anderson has averaged 10.1 points, 6.1 rebounds and 5.6 assists in 30.5 minutes of game-time, including racking up his first career triple-double with a 13 point, 11 rebound, 10 assist performance against the Utah Jazz. Magic-lite still doesn't play any defense and may have his minutes cut drastically when Avery Johnson returns this week but he most definitely made the most of his extended playing time and showed that he has a very bright future in this league.

At this point of the season LeBron James has a firm grip on the *MVP* trophy thanks to completely transforming the Cleveland Cavaliers from a laughing-stock into a juggernaut almost over-night. However, defending MVP Kevin Durant, thanks in large part to his league-leading 31.8 points per game is also a strong candidate, while Minnesota's Kevin Love is a serious dark-horse candidate as he is not only leading the league in rebounds but is third in scoring and has the Timberwolves firmly in line to make the playoffs for the first time in 11 seasons.

Anthony Davis of the New Orleans Pelicans also seems to have a stranglehold on the *Defensive Player of the Year* award, though LeBron James may get his fair share of votes for that award as well. Rajon Rondo is leading the league in assists as well, with Chris Paul and Ricky Rubio tied for second in that category.

With just 11 games remaining until All-Star Weekend, you receive a surprise phone call from Minnesota Timberwolves President of Basketball Operations Flip Saunders. Saunders was recently informed by Kevin Love's agent Jeff Schwartz that Love will not be exercising his team option for the 2015-16 season, will be testing free agency come the summer of 2015 and has no plans whatsoever to re-sign with the Timberwolves. Saunders is scared to death to lose Love for nothing the way the Orlando Magic lost Shaquille O'Neal in the summer of 96' and the Lakers lost Dwight Howard in the summer of 13' and has therefore offered to trade Kevin Love and his $15,719,063 expiring contract as well as J.J. Barea and his $4,519,500 expiring contract for rising star Julius Randle, backup point guard Greivis Vasquez and the expiring contract of reserve power forward Brandon Bass who combine to earn $15,983,320 this season, along with the Clippers 2015 first-round draft pick (obtained as compensation for former Celtics Coach Doc Rivers) and $3,000,000 cash.

You now have a very important decision to make. You could choose to stand pat with the Atlantic Division leading roster you currently have or you could choose to trade your *Rookie of the Year* candidate in Julius Randle along with Greivis Vasquez, Brandon Bass, a future first-round pick and $3,000,000 cash for MVP candidate Kevin Love and backup point guard J.J. Barea in the hope that Love will be the missing piece needed to return the Celtics to dominance and win an NBA title this season. Choose wisely.

If you would like to decline Flip Saunders offer and stand pat with your current roster, turn to page 96.

If you would like to trade Randle, Vasquez, Bass, the Clippers 2015 first-round pick and $3,000,000 cash for Kevin Love and J.J. Barea, turn to page 97.

Celtics CEO Wyc Grousbeck: *When you turned down Flip Saunders offer to trade Kevin Love and J.J. Barea for Julius Randle, Greivis Vasquez, Brandon Bass, the Clippers 2015 first-round pick and three-million cash, I flipped out. I started punching myself in the face so hard Danny Ainge thought I was Edward Norton in 'Fight Club'!*

After you decided to stand pat with your lineup we finished the season strong, winning 54 games and earning the fourth seed in the East; we even won our first round matchup with the Nets which was great. However, when we ran into LeBron James and the Cavs we got absolutely murdered!

You won a whopping total of four playoff games. I hired you to win four playoff series; Kevin Love could have helped us do that! I realize you love Julius Randle and think he may be a better player than Kevin Love within five years; however I didn't hire you to win a title in five years, I hired you to win a title now. Love's ability to score in a myriad of ways would have been far more valuable than watching Randle get his shot blocked time and time again, trying to bully his way to points against experienced defenders. You failed and now you're fired!

You're journey has ended.
Enjoy being an armchair GM.

Words of Wisdom:

Over the years I've had hundreds of shots blocked.

- John Havlicek

Celtics CEO Wyc Grousbeck: *I can't believe this; Kevin Love is a Celtic! That is unbelievable, just unbelievable!*

Words can't even express how insanely ecstatic I am right now. If MVP voters didn't ridiculously factor in team success into their choice, Kevin Love would have finished 3rd in the MVP race last year. The guy is a superstar who has gotten better every single year he's been in the league. He came into the NBA as a chubby big man who rebounded like mad and is now the most deadly stretch-4 the game has ever seen and still rebounds like mad. He's also known as an incredibly hard worker who will do whatever it takes to win. The guy is just a stud and now he's a Celtics stud, woo-hoo!

Great job! If I wouldn't have given you the title or bust ultimatum I would lock you up to a long-term contract right now. However, I did give you the title or bust ultimatum and I definitely expect a title now that we have K-Love. I also expect you to be able to re-sign him this coming off-season and not let him go sign with the Lakers as some pundits feel has been his plan all along. However, we'll cross that bridge when we come to it. For now, I will simply say, congrats, and look forward to the rest of the season!

Continue on to page 98.

After trading for Kevin Love, your Celtics won 10 of their next 11 games heading into the All-Star break and stood just .5 games behind the Chicago Bulls for the third seed in the Eastern Conference. However, the one game they lost after acquiring Love was to LeBron James' Cleveland Cavaliers, a game in which James himself went off for 51 points, torturing Jeff Green, Kyle Anderson and whoever else Celtics Coach Brad Stevens threw at him.

While your Celtics look like a strong contender to nab the third seed in the East, they still may not be good enough to even make a Conference Finals appearance, let alone win the NBA title. You have a lot of thinking to do.

ALL-STAR WEEKEND

The Eastern and Western Conference All-Star rosters this season are as follows:

Eastern Conference

Coach:	John Calipari
Starting Guard:	Derrick Rose
Starting Guard:	Kyrie Irving
Starting Forward:	Paul George
Starting Forward:	Carmelo Anthony
Starting Forward:	LeBron James
Backup Guard:	Goran Dragic
Backup Guard:	Dwyane Wade
Backup Forward:	Kevin Love
Backup Forward:	Al Jefferson
Backup Forward:	Joakim Noah
Reserve:	John Wall
Reserve:	Andre Drummond

Saving the Celtics

Western Conference

Coach:	Kevin McHale
Starting Guard:	Chris Paul
Starting Guard:	Kobe Bryant
Starting Forward:	Kevin Durant
Starting Forward:	Blake Griffin
Starting Forward:	Anthony Davis
Backup Guard:	Russell Westbrook
Backup Guard:	James Harden
Backup Forward:	LaMarcus Aldridge
Backup Forward:	Dirk Nowitzki
Backup Forward:	DeMarcus Cousins
Reserve:	Stephen Curry
Reserve:	Eric Bledsoe

Goran Dragic was the only member of the Celtics to make the All-Star team this season. However, Dragic played a large part in helping the East beat the West 132-128 behind an MVP performance from Derrick Rose who tallied 28 points and 6 assists, while chipping in 17 points (including five 3-pointers) and 7 assists himself.

You are now ready for the second half of the NBA season. However, before you leave New York City and return home to Boston to prepare for the rest of the season, you might want to answer your cell phone.

Golden State Warriors General Manager Bob Myers: Hello, this is Bob Myers. Listen, I know Wyc Grousbeck gave you a win-a-title-or-bust ultimatum and I watched your game against the Cavs the other night. You and I both know there is just no way you're going to beat the Cavs in a series without an elite defender on LeBron James; the guy just obliterated Jeff Green and Kyle Anderson in that game.

Anyways, we've got a little issue with our salary cap position going forward as we know we're going to have to give big bucks to Klay Thompson next year and even Draymond Green is going to get a huge raise from what we're paying him this year, and we'd like to be able to extend David Lee before he becomes a free agent. And you, you've got a major issue with your lack of defense at the small forward position. That said, I think we're the perfect trading partners and I want to propose a trade to you.

I don't have time to play games and I am making the absolute best offer I will ever make right now, especially considering that this is a three-team trade offer that includes the Memphis Grizzlies, and I'm not going back and forth with Chris 'The Celtics fired me so I gave the Lakers Pau Gasol to exact my revenge' Wallace, and Chris Wallace has already agreed to this deal as well. So, you can either take it or leave it but I won't listen to any silly counter-offers.

Anyways, you will receive Andre Iguodala and Jon Leur in exchange for Jeff Green and Kyle Anderson. We will be sending some cash and a future second round pick to the Grizzlies while acquiring the expiring contracts of both Tayshaun Prince and Kosta Koufos along with rookie Kyle Anderson. The Grizzlies will be the ones taking back Jeff Green's contract as well as receiving our cash and future second round pick.

Of course, what we and the Grizzlies are losing and receiving is none of your concern. You will be getting one of the best wing defenders as well as an utterly unselfish point-forward in Andre Iguodala, and the up-and-coming stretch-four Jon Leur for Jeff Green and Kyle Anderson. Personally, I think the trade is a no-brainer for you and that it makes sense for us. Ass for the Grizzlies, who cares? Chris Wallace is their GM and it was fun playing mind-games on him as he's not the brightest bulb in the box and I came away feeling like Einstein after convincing him to accept this deal, though in all seriousness, Jeff Green is a fine player and I doubt the Grizzlies had Tayshaun Prince in their long-term plans anyhow.

So, that's my offer and I want your answer right this second. So, what's it gonna be? Do we have a deal or not?

If you agree to trade Jeff Green and Kyle Anderson for
Andre Iguodala and Jon Leur,
turn to page 103.

If you decline Bob Myers trade offer,
turn to page 104.

Celtics CEO Wyc Grousbeck: *Wow, pulling the trigger on that trade took some real guts. I'm sad to see Jeff Green go. He's a fine young man and a quality starting small forward in this league. I'm also a little nervous about losing Kyle Anderson. I don't think he would have made the difference in us winning a ring this year or not as he's only a rookie and like most rookies is extremely inconsistent. However, the kid has the look of a future star and I wish we could have held onto him for the long-term.*

However, you've got to give up something good to get something good, and Andre Iguodala is definitely 'good'. I've always been a huge fan of Iggy's game. The guy is just a baller. It doesn't matter if you stick him at the point, shooting guard or small forward spots, or even if you have him defend stretch-fours, the guy just gets the job done.

This was a great trade in my book and one that definitely gets us closer to winning th NBA title this year! I can't wait to play the Cavaliers in the playoffs now; great work!

Continue on to page 105.

Celtics CEO Wyc Grousbeck: *When you turned down Bob Myers offer to trade Jeff Green and Kyle Anderson for Andre Iguodala and Jon Leur I was flabbergasted. You had just watched LeBron James utterly obliterate both Green and Anderson and had to have known there was no way we could possibly beat the Cavaliers in a series. If you didn't, you're even crazier than you look!*

After you decided to stand pat with your Kevin Love led lineup we finished the season strong, winning 58 games and earning the third seed in the East; we even won our first round matchup with the Raptors and then squeaked past the Bulls in the semi-finals which was awesome. But, then we ran into LeBron and the Cavs. We got humiliated and lost the series in just five games.

You should have pulled the trigger and acquired Andre Iguodala. You didn't. You failed, and now, you're fired!

You're journey has ended.
Enjoy being an armchair GM.

Words of Wisdom:

The idea is not to block every shot. The idea is to make your opponent believe that you might block every shot.

- Bill Russell

After trading for Andre Iguodala, your Celtics had just two games to play before the NBA Trade Deadline, one against the Chicago Bulls, a team you were battling with to earn the third seed in the East, and the Indiana Pacers, a team who was just ahead of you in the second seed. Your Celtics lost both games.

While newly acquired Andre Iguodala played fantastic all-around basketball, recently acquired Kevin Love got in foul trouble in both games, and with Jared Sullinger serving a two game suspension for striking the Pistons Josh Smith in the final game before the All-Star break, Kelly Olynyk, Channing Frye and Jon Leur got absolutely dominated in the paint and on the boards by Joakim Noah, Roy Hibbert and the Bulls and Pacers bevy of big-men. First the Bulls beat your Celtics 105-98 and then the Pacers beat down your Celtics 103-84.

Once again, you have a lot of thinking to do. And, with the trade deadline less than 24 hours away, not much time to do it.

TRADE DEADLINE

After acquiring Kevin Love, Andre Iguodala and Jon Leur your current roster is as follows:

Starting Point Guard:	Goran Dragic	$7,500,000
Starting Shooting Guard:	Gordon Hayward	$9,367,682
Starting Small Forward:	A. Iguodal	$12,289,544
Starting Power Forward:	Kevin Love	$15,719,063
Starting Center:	Kelly Olynyk	$2,075,760
Backup Point Guard:	J.J. Barea	$4,519,500
Backup Shooting Guard:	Avery Bradley	$5,217,391
Backup Small Forward:	Christa. Johnson	$915,243
Backup Power Forward:	Jared Sullinger	$1,424,520
Backup Center:	Channing Frye	$6,800,000
11th Man:	Jon Leur	$915,243
12th Man:	Joel Anthony	$3,800,000
13th Man:	Phil Pressey	$816,482
14th Man:	Chris Babb	$816,482
Total Team Salary:		$72,176,910

Led by the season-long magnificent point guard play of Goran Dragic, the all-around play of Gordan Hayward, the dominance of newly acquired Kevin Love, and perhaps the best bench in the NBA led by Jared Sullinger, Greivis Vasquez and Avery Bradley, not to mention the masterful coaching of Brad

Stevens, your Celtics sat at atop the Atlantic Division at 36-18 and were in line to earn the Eastern Conference's third seed. However, after losing their last two games to Conference rivals, you believed some tinkering may be called for.

The Cleveland Cavaliers, led by LeBron James and Kyrie Irving, have continued to steamroll the competition. They now have a full 7.0 game lead on your Celtics, as well as a full 4.0 game lead on the Indiana Pacers for the best record in the East, and a 1.5 game lead on Kevin Durant and Russell Westbrook's Oklahoma City Thunder squad for the best record in the NBA.

The good news is that not one single player on the Celtics roster has been a disappointment to date. While Goran Dragic and Kevin Love have been dominant and Andre Iguodala and Gordon Hayward have proved to be magnificent all-around players and teammates, starting center Kelly Olynyk has played far better as a sophomore than he did as a rookie as well. And, the bench mob, led by Jared Sullinger and his remarkable 13.7 points and 8.6 rebounds and Avery Bradley and his ball-hawking defense, have also taken the NBA by storm and proved to be huge advantage for your Celtics against just about every team in the league.

However, if there has been one single player that has seemed to be a harbinger of whether the Celtics will win or lose a particular game based on his individual play, it has far and away been second year man and starting center Kelly Olynyk. Olynyk has served as the team's de facto point-center this season and has become one of the best passing centers in the league today. He has also become the team's second leading rebounder, inching ahead of Jared Sullinger.

However, despite all of Olynyk's obvious gifts and contributions, he has been wildly inconsistent and also shown a penchant to get dominated in the paint and on the boards by the league's best centers. A prime example of this was the last two games your team played against Roy Hibbert's Indiana Pacers and Joakim Noah's Chicago Bulls. In those two games alone, Hibbert and Noah combined to average 20.0 points, 19.0 rebounds and 6.0 blocks per game! Olynyk on the other hand combined to average just 7.5 points, 6.5 rebounds and .5 blocks in those games, despite playing a total of 82 minutes over the two games!

An over-simplified statement would be that Olynyk is simply a young player and is therefore inconsistent and should not expected to be otherwise. However, the real truth may be that Olynyk simply is able to score and rebound at solid clips against smaller and/or inferior defenders while he cannot help but be dominated by the better centers in the game today. If such is the case, this could be an enormous problem come playoff time.

All of the above said, there are now less than 24 hours left until the *NBA Trade Deadline* passes. As your Celtics are not in the luxury tax and your current team salary is just $72,176.910 you have the ability to acquire incoming salaries that are up to 150% plus $100,000 more than the salaries of the players you trade, if the salaries of the players you trade are under $9,800,000 (Ex: If you trade players that make $2,000,000 you may receive players that make up to $3,100,000 in salary). If the salaries of the players you are trading are greater than $9,800,000 you may receive players with salaries up to $4,823,090 higher (normally $5,000,000 but you are just $4,823,090 away from the Luxury Tax threshold) than the combined salaries of what you are trading away (Ex: If you trade players that make $10,000,000 you may receive players that make up to $14,823,090 in salary). Simply put, you have options and options are always a good thing.

At this point you have let each and every GM across the league know that you are *open for business*, going all-in to a win a championship this season and that you will consider any trade that will give the Celtics a better shot to win a ring this season. However, various General Managers across the league have already let you know in no uncertain terms that they have no desire to help you in your quest and will not be submitting any trade proposals to you whatsoever.

Many other GM's submitted at least one trade proposal to you which you rejected out of hand as they were laughable and would have only served to decrease your chances of winning a title this season. There are three trade proposals that you feel merit serious consideration though, any one or more of which you could choose to pull the trigger on. However, please be aware that these trade decisions are the last move(s) you will make roster-wise that will directly affect the team's on-court performance this season.

You can choose to stand pat and trust the team you have assembled so far and see what Coach Stevens can do with such a roster. Or, you can pull the trigger on one of the following three trade proposals. Choose wisely.

Proposal One: Houston Rockets General Manager Daryl Morey has offered to trade Omer Asik and his $14,898,938 expiring contract, as well as Francisco Garcia and his $1,316,809 expiring contract for Jared Sullinger and the expiring contracts of Channing Frye and Joel Anthony who earn a combined $12,024,520.

Proposal Two: New York Knicks Grand Poobah Phil Jackson has offered to trade Tyson Chandler and his $14,596,888 expiring contract, as well as Iman Shumpert and his $2,761,113 expiring contract for Jared Sullinger and the expiring contracts of Channing Frye and Joel Anthony who earn a combined $12,024,520.

Proposal Three: Los Angeles Lakers General Manager Mitch Kupchak has offered to trade Kobe Bryant and the expiring contracts of Robert Sacre and Kendall Marshall who combine to make $25,330,486 this season for Kevin Love, Gordon Hayward and Greivis Vasquez who earn a combined $29,086,745.

If you would like to stand pat,
turn to page 112.

If you would like to trade Sullinger, Frye and Anthony to the Rockets for Omer Asik and Francisco Garcia,
turn to page 113.

If you would like to trade Sullinger, Frye and Anthony to the Knicks for Tyson Chandler and Iman Shumpert,
turn to page 114.

If you would like to trade Love, Hayward and Vazquez to the Los Angeles Lakers for Kobe Bryant, Robert Sacre and Kendall Marshall,
turn to page 115.

Celtics CEO Wyc Grousbeck: *You believed in the roster you had built and stood pat and I respected that. We even finished the year winning an insane 24 out of 28 games and with a 60-22 record which earned us the second seed in the East. We then swept the Charlotte Bobcats in the first round and won a no-holds-barred seven game series against the Indiana Pacers in the second round. By that time I couldn't wait for us to play the Cavs and slap LeBron James around and we did! I mean, I guess his severe lower ankle sprain had a little something to do with us winning but I don't care. We knocked the Cavs out and advanced to the Finals against the Houston Rockets and I was sure we were about to win our 18th franchise title. I was wrong.*

The Rockets pounded up inside the entire series. Dwight Howard dominated each and every game on his way to winning Finals MVP and even back-up center Omer Asik dominated us when he was on the floor as well. It wasn't pretty.

You won an Eastern Conference title in your first year; congrats. However, you didn't win me a ring; you're fired!

You're journey has ended.
Enjoy being an armchair GM.

Words of Wisdom:

The only correct actions are those that demand no explanation and no apology.

- Red Aeurbach

Celtics CEO Wyc Grousbeck: *Nice trade! I'm sad to see Jared Sullinger go but he wasn't getting as much playing time as he used to anyways with Kevin Love on the team. Besides, Kelly Olynyk can pick up some minutes at the power forward and even Jon Leur can actually play and is a capable back-up four; who knew?*

Anyways, after we got destroyed by the Pacers and Bulls recently, with Olynyk getting dominated down low by Roy Hibbert and Joakim Noah, I knew we needed a defensive minded center with length and the ability to rebound like a mad-man and not care about his 'touches' on the offensive end, as you know with Dragic, Love, Hayward and Iggy around there's no touches for a center anyways, hahaha. That said, I'm not sure there was another center in the in the entire NBA that fits the bill as well as Omer Asik does. He is exactly what this team needs and I am thrilled with this trade!

You have earned my respect and trust and I am thrilled I hired you. Now, go win me a ring while I make preparations for the Championship Parade!

Continue on to page 117.

Author Bryant T. Jordan: *That would have been a great trade huh? Nabbing both Tyson Chandler and Iman Shumpert for Sully, Frye and Joel Anthony seemed like a no-brainer didn't it.*

However, choosing this option simply proves you don't have what it takes to be an NBA General Manager as you obviously have a problem paying attention to detail. I made it very clear that the absolute maximum you could take back in additional salary was $4,823,090. Now, you tell me what $14,596,888 (Tyson Chandler's salary) plus $2,761,113 (Iman Shumpert's salary) is? That's right, it's $17,358,001.

Now, you tell me what $17,358,001 minus $12,024,520 (the combined outgoing salaries of Sullinger, Frye and Anthony) is? That's right again, it's $5,333,481.

Now, you tell me if $5,333,481 is more or less than $4,823,090? That's right again, it's more, which means you just tried to execute a trade that isn't even possible under the current Collective Bargaining Agreement!

I'm not Celtics CEO Wyc Grousbeck so I won't fire you. You can go back to Page 112 and try again, but this time, check those digits baby! And, by the way, go buy a copy of my 'Saving the Lakers: A Be the General Manager Book' as well. I could use the loot.

Words of Wisdom:

Check those digits baby!

- Bryant T. Jordan

Celtics CEO Wyc Grousbeck: *Really? Really!*

Why don't you go and buy a copy of Bryant T. Jordan's 'Saving the Lakers: A Be the General Manager Book' as you obviously would rather be the Lakers GM than the GM of the Celtics. Who knows, maybe Jimmy Buss will hire you, but there's no way you're getting a good reference from me!

I'm not even going to let you finish out this season. If you want to sue me, sue me, but you are fired! Now get out of my office and don't ever show your face in Boston again!

You're journey has ended.
Enjoy being an armchair GM.

Words of Wisdom:

I have self-doubt. I have insecurity. I have fear of failure. I have nights when I show up at the arena and I'm like, 'My back hurts, my feet hurt, my knees hurt. I don't have it. I just want to chill.' We all have self-doubt. You don't deny it, but you also don't capitulate to it. You embrace it.

- Kobe Bryant

THE FRUITS OF YOUR LABOR

Your Boston Celtics 2014-15 roster is now 13 deep, set in stone, and as follows:

Starting Point Guard:	Goran Dragic	$7,500,000
Starting Shooting Guard:	Gordon Hayward	$9,367,682
Starting Small Forward:	A. Iguodala	$12,289,544
Starting Power Forward:	Kevin Love	$15,719,063
Starting Center:	Omer Asik	$14,898,938
Backup Point Guard:	Greivis Vasquez	$4,519,500
Backup Shooting Guard:	Avery Bradley	$5,217,391
Backup Small Forward:	Francisco Garcia	$1,316,809
Backup Power Forward:	Jon Leur	$967,500
Backup Center:	Kelly Olynyk	$2,075,760
11th Man:	Christa. Johnson	$915,243
12th Man:	Phil Pressey	$816,482
13th Man:	Chris Babb	$816,482
Total Team Salary:		$76,420,394

After making the extremely gutsy decision to trade possible *6th Man of the Year* Jared Sullinger, solid back-up power forward and stretch-four Channing Frye and reserve veteran center Joel Anthony, not to mention electing to bench starting center and possible *Most Improved Player* Kelly Olynyk, for the Houston Rockets Omer Asik and back-up small forward Francisco Garcia, the potential for disaster was huge. However, the potential for epic success was also huge and with a title or bust ultimatum, swinging for the fences made more sense than taking ball four and walking it out.

Swapping three players for two may have reduced the team's depth a bit, if Joel Anthony ever played that is, which he did not. In fact, inserting Omer Asik into the starting lineup did wonders for the *first five* and gave them the defensive post presence and interior rebounder they sorely lacked. And, moving former starting center Kelly Olynyk to the second unit gave the bench mob the dynamic post presence and legitimate center they had been missing. All things considered, the deadline trade did wonders for your entire team!

Omer Asik played a total of 28 games for the Celtics after being acquired in trade at the deadline. During those 28 games, Asik averaged 11.5 points, 13.1 rebounds and 2.1 blocks in 34.0 minutes per game. Kelly Olynyk, after the being moved to the back-up center position also increased his points, rebounds, steals, blocks and assists per-40 minutes and seemed to relish his new role as leader of the team's bench mob.

With Asik manning the paint and Olynyk leading the bench, the team's starting five became a much better defensive unit while the second unit became much more efficient offensively. Your Celtics won 24 of their final 28 games and locked up the second seed in the Eastern Conference after throttling the then-second-seed Indiana Pacers 101-79 during the final week of the regular season.

Needless to say, your Celtics entered the Playoffs with a 60-22 record and as the second seed in the Eastern Conference, behind only LeBron James and his Cleveland Cavaliers. Over in the West the Oklahoma City Thunder narrowly edged out the Houston Rockets for the top seed, despite Houston finishing the season on an 11 game win streak and embarrassing the Thunder 121-99 in Houston during the final week of the season.

In the first round of the playoffs your Celtics faced off against the young and talented Charlotte Bobcats led by All-Star center Al Jefferson and star point guard Kemba Walker. The Bobcats had entered the playoffs on a hot-streak winning nine of their last 10 games and beating out the Miami Heat for the seventh seed, thanks in large part to throttling the Heat in Miami 118-99 in the second to last game of the regular season. However, your Celtics were far too balanced, deep and experienced for the young Bobcats. Led by Kevin Love's 30.5 points and 12.5 rebounds per game, your Celtics swept the Bobcats, outscoring them by an average of 13.0 points per game, thanks to a 113-79 throttling in the fourth and final game.

In other Eastern Conference first round matchups the top seed of the entire playoffs, the Cleveland Cavaliers, absolutely drubbed the eighth seed Miami Heat in four straight games. LeBron James tortured his former team to the tune of averaging a triple double (27.5 points, 10.5 rebounds and 10.0 assists) while playing lock-down defense on former running mate Dwyane Wade who managed to shoot just 29% from the field for the series.

The third seed Indiana Pacers and sixth seed Toronto Raptors engaged in a heated six game series that ended with the Pacers celebrating a hard fought victory on the Raptors home court. The Raptors put up a great fight through-out the series, winning games three and four by a combined 22 points and losing games one and six by just a point apiece. However Paul George, Lance Stephenson and the Pacers depth and experience were far too much for the young Raptors to handle this time around.

The fourth seed Chicago Bulls and star point guard Derrick Rose faced off against the fifth seed Brooklyn Nets and their conglomeration of geriatric stars. The Nets Kevin Garnett had a series for the ages, making 34 of 38 field goal attempts he took as well as all 12 free throw attempts he took during the series, while finishing the series averaging 16 points and 10 rebounds. However, the Bulls dogged team defense coupled with the scoring outbursts of Rose and the all-around excellence of Joakim Noah were too much for the aged Nets to overcome as Chicago won the series in just 5 games.

Kevin Garnett announced his retirement after the fifth and final game of the series and shocked everyone by stating, *I've reached an agreement in principle to buy the Minnesota Timberwolves and plan to rename them the Frozen Sota Garnett's and erect no less than 12 bronze statues of myself out front, one for each season I played in Minny. When asked why he would do such a thing, Garnett replied by saying, What else am I going to do with all the money I made, buy 100 homes in Boston or 100,000 homes in Detroit? Nah, I want to own my own team!*

In Western Conference first round matchups the top seed Oklahoma City Thunder slaughtered the Los Angeles Lakers and their revamped lineup, winning four straight games by a combined total of 50 points. Kobe Bryant, Luol Deng, Pau Gasol and the elderly Lakers put up a very solid fight in the first and third games, losing on last second shots by Kevin Durant in both games. However, the Lakers realized they were outclassed after getting humiliated 111-78 in the second game of the series, despite Bryant's incredible 32 point, 10 rebound performance. Perhaps the Buss family should have read Bryant T. Jordan's ingenious *Saving the Lakers: A Be the General Manager Book* and followed his instructions!

The second seed Houston Rockets obliterated the seventh seed Dallas Mavericks in four straight games. won a tough six game series with the Dallas Mavericks. In the series' final game, Dwight Howard came up big with 19 points, 19 rebounds and 11 blocked shots while James Harden poured in 33 points to give the Rockets a 116-112 victory over the Mavs, who wasted Dirk Nowitzki's virtuoso 47 point performance.

The third seed Los Angeles Clippers and sixth seed Golden State Warriors met in what was easily the most entertaining and even matchup of the first round. The series came down to an overtime period in the seventh and final game after Chris Paul hit a step-back jumper over the outstretched hand of Tayshaun Prince at the regulation buzzer. However, overtime belonged to Golden State's *Splash Brothers* as Stephen Curry and Klay Thompson each nailed two three- pointers and scored eight points as the Warriors won the deciding game 128-123.

The fourth seed San Antonio Spurs and fifth seed Portland Trailblazers also played one of the most memorable first round series in league history. The series featured four over-time periods, a buzzer-beating victory in the penultimate game in Portland and a Game Seven for the ages in San Antonio. The Trailblazers held an 87-77 lead going into the fourth quarter of the final game before the old, reliable trio of Tim Duncan, Tony Parker and Manu Ginobili turned up the Heat and used their masterful execution to rally past the Blazers and wrap up the series with a thrilling 107-106 victory, thanks to Tim Duncan block at the buzzer on a Robin Lopez put-back attempt.

The second round of the playoffs featured four great matchups including your Celtics facing off against Larry Bird's Indiana Pacers. The series was expected to be heated, with most talking heads predicting a Pacers victory in six games. However, your Celtics put on a clinic in Game One and blew the Pacers out of the TD Garden 103-74. Your Celtics eliminated the Pacers in just 5 games and served notice on the rest of the league that they were for real, and as the Dogfather of American Idol would say, in it to win it!

On the other side of the Eastern Conference bracket, the Cleveland Cavaliers made quick work of the Chicago Bulls, sweeping them in four straight games behind LeBron James second straight series averaging a triple double and the offensive wizardry of Kyrie Irving. James averaged 25.5 points, 10.5 rebounds and 10.5 assists while Irving torched Derrick Rose, averaging 29.5 points per game.

In the Western Conference the top seed Oklahoma City Thunder brought a violent end to the career of Tim Duncan who was playing his final season with the San Antonio Spurs. The Thunder destroyed the Spurs, sweeping the series and outscoring them by a total of 64 points. Duncan had little impact on the series averaging just 9.5 points and 6.5 rebounds while Kevin Durant and Russell Westbrook each averaged over 28 points per game for the high-scoring Thunder.

After the series and ultimately his playing career hand ended, Tim Duncan held a press conference and announced that he was going to offer to become the next General Manager of the Milwaukee Bucks. When asked if they had offered him such a position, he replied by saying, *No. They haven't. However, that doesn't make any difference. They suck. They need me. They haven't been relevant since Lew Alcindor was playing there. So, I'm just making it known here and now that I am prepared to take over their sorry franchise and return it to glory.* San Antonio Express-News sports columnist Buck Harvey quickly asked, *Tim, this is very unlike you. Are you sure you're not joking? Maybe Pop's dry wit has rubbed off on you",* to which Duncan answered, *No, I'm not joking Buck. I've played the nice little Spur for far too long. Everyone expected me to go about my business silently and just be a model citizen and that's what Pop expected of me, so that's what I did. However, I'm retired now, I'm no longer a Spur and therefore I finally get to be myself. So, that's what I'm doing. I want to run the Milwaukee Bucks and they would be off their rockers not to hire me. I'm going to fire the coach, GM and trade away most of the players on that awful roster, but I will remake it into a champion!*

On the other side of the Western Conference bracket, the second seed Houston Rockets and MVP candidate James Harden absolutely dismantled the Golden State Warriors in four straight games, sweeping them put of the playoffs with a 129-108 victory in the fourth and final game. The Warriors Stephen Curry had a monster series averaging 33.5 points and 8.5 assists per game but it was Dwight Howard and his 24 point and 18 rebound series averages that devastated the Warriors and crushed their hopes of advancing to the Conference Finals.

During the second round of the Playoffs the league announced its individual award winners, which were as follows:

Most Valuable Player:	LeBron James (Cavs)
Defensive Player of the Year:	LeBron James (Cavs)
Sixth Man of the Year:	Tyreke Evans (Pelicans)
Most Improved Player:	Anthony Bennett (Cavs)

Comeback Player of the Year: Kobe Bryant (Lakers)

Rookie of the Year: Andrew Wiggins (Bucks)

Coach of the Year: Brad Stevens (Celtics)

Your Celtics were well represented in the various award races with Coach Brad Stevens winning the *Coach of the Year* award, Kelly Olynyk finishing second in the *Most Improved Player* award and Kevin Love finishing third in the *Most Valuable Player* race behind only 2013 *MVP* Kevin Durant and winner and five-time *MVP* LeBron James. Goran Dragic also finished tenth in the *MVP* race as well. However, your Celtics were built to win the *Larry O'Brien Championship Trophy* and not merely individual awards.

The Conference Finals are now up for grabs and each Conference's top two seeds will be playing for the right to battle in the NBA Finals:

Your Celtics squared off with *MVP* LeBron James, super star point guard Kyrie Irving and the dominant Cleveland Cavaliers. It was obvious from the start of the series that LeBron James was hell bent on destroying your Celtics and cementing himself on his own personal NBA Mount Rushmore. James took flak from many talking heads and even from the great Celtic Bill Russell when he left the 11-time NBA champion off his personal Mount Rushmore list during a 2014 interview, a list that featured Michael Jordan, Magic Johnson, Larry Bird and Oscar Robertson. Regardless, LeBron James was on his own personal quest to surpass at the very least Oscar Robertson, if not both Larry Bird and Magic Johnson, and to firmly set himself on his own personal NBA Mount Rushmore alongside Michael Jordan and whoever else anyone wants to throw up their as the third and fourth all-time greats.

Eastern Conference Finals Game One: Game One looked like a reenactment of the 1770 Boston Massacre, with LeBron James playing the role of King George III and Kyrie Irving playing the role of Private Hugh Montgomery and firing the first shot at the hapless Celtic bystanders. When the second quarter buzzer sounded LeBron James had already racked up a triple double with 21 points, 11 rebounds and 10 assists and Kyrie Irving had poured in a game high 23 points on 9-14 from the field. The Cavaliers held a 70-39 lead.

After receiving the most severe tongue lashing they had received since their mama's scolded them for talking in church, from Coach Brad Stevens during halftime, the Celtics started the third quarter with a renewed dedication to unselfish offense and dynamic team defense. However, after the first six minutes of the third quarter your Celtics had reduced the 31 point deficit by just four points and were still trailing 79-52. LeBron James had scored all nine of the Cavaliers third qu quarter points and seemed as if he could have held your Celtics at bay and secured the win playing with little more than a JV High School team as running mates. Then, it happened.

After Kyrie Irving missed a deep three-pointer from the right corner and Kevin Love corralled the rebound and fired one of his QB-esque passes to a streaking Greivis Vasquez, LeBron James turned on his heels and proceeded to chase down Vasquez from behind. As Vasquez leapt to drop in a finger roll, LeBron elevated. Just as the ball rolled off the tips of Vasquez's fingers, James hand swatted it into the third row of the stands. However, as James landed, his left ankle snapped. As James lay on the *Quicken Loans Arena* floor, writhing in pain, obviously out for the rest of the season, the hopes of Cavaliers fans everywhere faded into oblivion.

With just 17 minutes remaining in the game and the Cavaliers still ahead 79-52 Cleveland fell apart in front of the masses. Without their two-time franchise savior the Cavaliers looked hapless on offense, relying on little more than running isolation after isolation play for Kyrie Irving, without much success. Your Celtics on the other hand caught fire.

With Andre Iguodala hounding Kyrie Irving on the defensive end and Goran Dragic torching Irving on the offensive end, as well as Kevin Love utterly dominating whoever the Cavaliers threw at him, your Celtics finished the third quarter on a 20-7 run and trailed 86-72 going into the fourth quarter. The fourth quarter was more of the same as your Celtics outscored the Cavaliers 35-17 and won the game 107-103. In fact, after LeBron James went down with a broken ankle, your Celtics outscored the Cavaliers 55-24, pulling out one of the largest come from behind victories in NBA history.

Eastern Conference Finals Game Two: Game Two started much the same way as Game One, just in reverse, with your Celtics jumping all over the ill-fated Cavaliers and marching into half time with a 61-29 lead. However, while Game One featured one of the greatest comebacks in NBA history, Game Two simply featured a good ole fashion, wire-to-wire butt whooping. When the final buzzer sounded, the scoreboard read Celtics 112 - Cavaliers 59.

Eastern Conference Finals Game Three: Game Three was in Boston and while your Celtics were expected to win in yet another route, Kyrie Irving and the Cavaliers played their heart out from the opening tip and made an game of it. Irving especially seemed more than ready to carry his team to the NBA Finals as he poured in 17 points in the first quarter, 10 points in the second and 11 points in the third. However, your Celtics held an 82-78 lead entering the final quarter.

Irving continued his torrid scoring in the final quarter, pouring in another 12 points and finishing the game with 50 points on 17-31 from the field. However, it was the scoring of Kevin Love (37 points), passing of Goran Dragic (14 assists), rebounding of Omer Asik (19 rebounds) and all-around excellence of Andre Iguodala (10 points, 10 rebounds, 10 assists, 5 steals, 3 blocks and 0 turnovers on 4-4 shooting) that earned a hard fought 106-102 victory for your Boston Celtics.

Eastern Conference Finals Game Four: Game Four was a laugher, period. It looked as if the Cavaliers entire roster, coaching staff and ball boys knew the team had no chance of coming back and winning four straight games, and therefore decided to just mentally check out. Your Celtics cruised to an easy 112-89 victory and a series sweep of the LeBron-less Cavaliers.

Kyrie Irving finished the series averaging 40.5 points and 6.5 assists for the Cavaliers. However, it was Kevin Love who finished the series averaging 31.5 points, 12.8 rebounds and 4.3 assists per game, all while hitting on just over 60 percent of his field goal attempts, that had one of the greatest Eastern Conference Finals performances ever and led his squad to the NBA Finals.

In the Western Conference Finals the top seed Oklahoma City Thunder faced off against the Houston Rockets and former running mate James Harden. The dynamic duo of Kevin Durant and Russell Westbrook were more than up for the challenge the hot Rockets, winners of 19 straight games, threw at them.

While James Harden and Dwight Howard played fantastic all-around basketball and sharp-shooting swingman Chandler Parsons shot the lights out from the perimeter, it was Durant and Westbrook that controlled the series. Durant was unstoppable on the offensive end, pouring in a series leading 31.5 points per game, while Westbrook did a little bit of everything in averaging 25.5 points, 7.5 assists, 6.5 rebounds and 2.5 steals, in leading the Thunder to an unexpected and rather frightening series sweep of the powerful Rockets.

Kevin Durant and Russell Westbrook were both playing the best ball of their careers. The Thunder's young stallions had become the most dominant duo the NBA had seen since Kobe Bryant and Shaquille O'Neal won four Western Conference titles (as well as three NBA championship rings) in five years from 2000-2004. However, unlike Kobe and Shaq, Kevin and Russell seemed to get along like bosom buddies and have a solid ten plus seasons of dominance still in front of them.

The Thunder entered the NBA Finals as the prohibitive favorites after posting a 68-14 regular season record and perfect 12-0 record throughout the Western Conference Playoffs. Your Celtics entered the NBA Finals coming off an utter dismantling and unexpected sweep of the Cleveland Cavaliers and had had finished the regular season 60-22 and the rolled through the Eastern Conference playoffs posting a 12-1 record as well.

Before the series started Kevin Durant and Russell Westbrook were interviewed by ESPN's Bill Simmons who asked what beating the Celtics in a championship series would mean for each player's respective legacy. Durant replied, *Oh man, it would be sweet. I mean, it's not like the Celtics are just another team. They've won 17 titles and have been involved in some of the greatest Finals series in history. Winning a title against Boston would be awesome. But, it's in the Lord hands. I'm going to play my best and do what I can to win this thing but it's in the Lord's hands.* Westbrook replied by saying, *Man, I don't care who I have to beat to win the ring, I just want to win the ring. It will be sweet slapping around Kevin Love and Omer Asik though, I'll say that. Kevin and I played at UCLA together and I always thought that cat got too much press, hah-hah-hah. As for Asik, I seriously want to slap him. He played on the same team as that little punk Patrick Beverley and while he may not have condoned that little test-cheater and D-leaguer's bush-league play when he knee-capped me, he didn't speak out against it either. By the time this series is over, not only will I be holding the Larry O'Brien trophy but I will have posterized Asik a few times and made him look like the goof-ball he is!*

When told of the Durant's and Westbrook's comments by Bill Simmons during a pre-Finals interview, Kevin Love responded, *Durant's a good dude ma and Wes is my boy; I don't want to start a war of words or anything. Honestly, it wouldn't shock me if he did posterize Omer a few times. However, he shouldn't be surprised if Omer sends him packing a few times too. Omer can play man, he's a legit center and doesn't get enough credit for everything he means to this team. People want to make him out to be our Kendrick Perkins but honestly Perkins can't hold a candle to Asik. And honestly, while KD and Russ are great, I don't think the Thunder's team is as well-built as ours. We're going to win this thing, just wait and see.*

Bill Simmons chuckled and said, *Kevin, you might not want to talk smack about the Thunder. They could be the best team the NBA has seen since the Bird, McHale and Parish Celtics!* Love smirked and said, *I mean, I respect the Thunder and only God knows what's going to happen for sure, but I just love our team. We've got one of the best point guards and small forwards on the planet, maybe the best true center in the NBA, a seriously under-rated shooting guard in Hayward and the best bench in the league without a doubt. We've got a great squad and in my mind, we are the team to beat. I don't care what anyone else thinks.*

Bill Simmons nodded before saying, *Okay, okay. Let me ask you one more question. If you do win this series and earn your first ring, beating one of the greatest player's the game has ever seen in Durant, where will that put you in terms of the best players in the game or even on the all-time power forwards list?* Love shakes his head and chuckles before saying, *You know what. I already feel like I'm a top three player in this league and winning or losing this series won't change that. But, as far as where I will rank on an all-time power forward list, that's interesting; I guess I would rank myself second, behind only Duncan. I mean, come on, how can I rank myself behind someone like Barkley or Karl Malone when they never won even one ring? I suppose I could be behind Kevin Garnett and Dirk Nowitzki until I get my second ring, but I'm not going to be the one to say that.*

The Finals were set and it seemed no one could get enough news, coverage, gossip and predictions. Magic Johnson believed the Thunder would win the series in 5 games or less. Larry Bird felt the Celtics had a shot to win the series if the could steal Game One but said he wouldn't bet against Kevin Durant. And, Michael Jordan himself said he'd be shocked if the Thunder didn't sweep your Celtics. In fact, Vegas odds-makers had the Thunder as prohibitive favorite to win the Finals and even odds to sweep your Celtics as well. However, as Buster Douglas and Mike Tyson know, Vegas isn't always right.

NBA Finals Game One: Game One resembled a heavyweight boxing match with both teams seemingly feeling each other out and taking it slow in the first quarter and four minutes or so of the second. When most of the starters checked back in for both sides with about 8 minutes to go in the first half, the teams were deadlocked 33-33. However, in the last 8 minutes of the first half Kevin Love caught fire; the player some consider the 21st century version of Larry Bird (or at least a better rebounding version of Dirk Nowitzki) scored 13 points in the last 8 minutes of the half and the Celtics went into the locker room with a 51-48 lead.

The third quarter was more of the same; neither team pulled ahead and each team's superstars (Love and Dragic as well as Durant and Westbrook) shouldered the load offensively. The third quarter ended with the Celtics up 76-75.

The first four minutes of the fourth quarter were disastrous for the Celtics. With both Kevin Love and Goran Dragic on the bench and Kevin Durant and Russell Westbrook staying on the court the Thunder outscored the Celtics 10-4; when Dragic and Love checked back into the game the Celtics were behind 85-80 with just 8 minutes to play.

Over the next 8 minutes Kevin Durant played the role of facilitator with teammate Russell Westbrook being the prime benefactor, while the Celtics relied on Goran Dragic to bail them out time and time again with the shot clock running down after the Thunder had stifled their attempts at quick buckets. With just 58 seconds left in the game and the Thunder ahead 97-95 Kevin Durant held the ball at the top of the key. He feigned left and then took a couple of dribbles to the right before shooting a fall away jumper over Andre Iguodala that clanged off the right side of the rim and into the hands of Kevin Love. Love quickly flipped the ball to Goran Dragic who took no more than two dribbles before zipping a beautiful cross-court bounce pass to Gordon Hayward for a wide-open three pointer that swished through the net giving the Celtics a 98-97 lead with 28 seconds remaining.

After Thunder Coach Scott Brooks' timeout, Kevin Durant inbounded the ball to Russell Westbrook who dribbled the shot clock down to 4 seconds before making his move to the basket. Westbrook got into the lane with ease, split two defenders and made a nice floater from 8 feet over Omer Asik to give the Thunder a one point lead with just five seconds left in the game.

After Celtics Coach Brad Stevens drew up the final play during a 20 second timeout Andre Iguodala inbounded the ball to Goran Dragic who had Russell Westbrook draped all over him. Dragic gave a quick pump fake, spun to his left, took two dribbles and started to rise for a fall-away jumper from 20'. However before releasing the shot, Dragic noticed Serge Ibaka flying at him from the left and leaving Kevin Love all alone just inside the three-point line. Dragic gave a flick of his left wrist and passed the ball to a wide open Love who let fly, burying the shot and giving the Celtics a 100-99 victory and a 1-0 lead in the series.

NBA Finals Game Two: The Oklahoma City Thunder looked like an entirely different team in Game Two. Gone was the overconfidence and nonchalant play they displayed in the first game. Kevin Durant and company were ready for a no-holds-barred street-fight this time around.

The Thunder quickly jumped on the Celtics, outscoring them 11-0 in the game's first 3 minutes en route to building a 35-19 lead at the end of the first quarter. The second quarter was better for the Celtics, though not by much, as they were outscored 27-20 and entered halftime down 62-39.

Goran Dragic, who had only shot the ball three times in the first half, missing all three attempts and scoring just 5 points on free throws, came out firing in the third quarter. The Dragon attempted to rekindle some of that first game magic in which he poured in 23 points. However, while Dragic scored a solid 14 points in the third quarter he needed 12 shots to do so and the Celtics entered the fourth quarter down 85-68.

Dragic stayed on the floor for the entire fourth quarter and continued his high-volume scoring act, adding 13 points on 11 shots. Dragic finished with 32 points on 26 shots while Kevin Durant managed to score 30 points on just 14 shots, thanks in large part to making 12 of 14 free-throws. Game Two went to the Thunder 106-97.

NBA Finals Game Three: Back in Boston the Celtics were actually expected to win Game Three and take a 2-1 series lead; however it was the Oklahoma City Thunder who looked like the home team, played with poise and took it to the Celtics from the opening tip. The entire game was one big stinker from start to finish for L.A. as Kevin Durant put on his usual high-scoring show, dropping 41 points while Russell Westbrook erupted for 30 points on just 17 shots, thanks to the six three-pointers he drained. Even defensive minded Serge Ibaka outscored Kevin Love 20-19.

When Serge Ibaka outscores Kevin Love, you can't expect to win many games. Game Three was no exception as the Thunder entirely annihilated the Celtics 109-78.

NBA Finals Game Four: The atmosphere was tense to start Game Four, not merely NBA Finals tense but one-and-done elimination tense, best friends fighting over a girl tense. Just 30 seconds into the game Russell Westbrook posterized Omer Asik and finished the highlight-reel play with a shove and scream. Less than two minutes later Omer Asik delivered a hard foul on Kevin Durant that left the star small forward bleeding from the right eye-brow.

By the time the first quarter buzzer sounded the teams had combined for twenty personal fouls, four technical fouls and just 38 points with the game tied 19-19. Andre Iguodala was the Celtics leading scorer with 7 points while Jeremy Lamb was the Thunder's leading scorer with 6 points.

The second quarter was played at a feverish pace and while just as heated as the first, the teams actually seemed capable of playing defense without trying to bludgeon or decapitate each other. At half-time the teams were knotted 43-43 and though it was still anyone's game one had the feeling that this was the Celtics game to lose, more than the Thunder's game to win. Durant and Westbrook each had three fouls and Westbrook could not find his shooting touch, hitting just 2-11 shots and scoring a total of 4 points.

The third quarter seemed to resemble the first in many ways, not the least of which was the *Inquisition* like bloodshed and maniacal tempers. Greivis Vasquez and Francisco Garcia were each ejected near the end of the third quarter with both throwing punches. Vasquez took a wild swing at Russell Westbrook who had shoved him from behind on a layup attempt while Garcia connected on a straight jab to the jaw of Kendrick Perkins who had first swung on him in the melee. The third quarter ended with the teams deadlocked at 77-77.

The fourth quarter started with a bang as Avery Johnson picked Reggie Jackson's pocket and fed Andre Iguodala for a thunderous slam over Thunder backup small forward Perry Jones III. The Celtics held a solid 6 point lead with just 5 minutes to play before Jeremy Lamb, who had been on fire all game, went on another scoring barrage. Lamb dropped 11 points over the next 4:30 of game time and tied the game up at 101 on a deep three-pointer drilled right in the face of Goran Dragic.

The final 30 seconds of game time seemed to last an entire quarter though there would be just two possessions. Russell Westbrook held the ball at the top of the key with the clock ticking down; Thunder Coach Scott Brooks had called for Jeremy Lamb to come off a screen and then to either take an open jumper along the left baseline or fire a quick pass back out to Westbrook or Durant if covered. The play actually worked exactly the way Coach Brooks wanted it too with Lamb coming off a Steven Adams screen and catching a pass along the left baseline and Goran Dragic a solid 6 feet away. However, as soon as Lamb caught the ball Andre Iguodala left Kevin Durant and closed out on Lamb faster than Twista spits lyrics; Iggy got just enough of the shot to make it fall a few feet short of the basket and into the waiting arms of Kevin Love who was always in the right place at the right time throughout the game.

After the Celtics called timeout with 11 seconds remaining in the game Coach Brad Stevens called for a simple isolation play, choosing to place the ball in Goran Dragic's capable hands and let him make the final decision of who shoots and from where. When Dragic got the ball he held it for a few seconds before making his move toward the right baseline. When he got to the baseline and it appeared he was going to go all the way to the rack and try to win the game himself, he quickly spun back towards the middle of court, took one dribble towards the free-throw line and jumped. Serge Ibaka was sure Dragic was shooting for the win, left his man and jumped out to block the shot just as Dragic threw a perfect, soft lob-pass toward the right side of the rim ... and into the hands of Kevin Love who caught the alley-oop and slammed it through the net as time expired. The Celtics won Game Four 103-101 to tie the series at 2-2.

NBA Finals Game Five: The teams returned to Oklahoma City tied at two games apiece and with both Greivis Vasquez and Francisco Garcia of the Celtics, as well as Kendrick Perkins of the Thunder, suspended due to their respective roles in the Game Four melee. Game Five would be more akin to a massacre than a melee as other than Kevin Love and Goran Dragic your Celtics didn't even bother to show up.

Love and Dragic poured in 27 points apiece; however their teammates combined to score just 35 points. The Thunder on the other hand had seven players in double figures, led by Kevin Durant with 24 points, and scoured an astounding 122 points to drub the Celtics by 33 points, 122-89.

NBA Finals Game Six: Back in Boston for Game Six your Celtics found themselves in their first win-or-go-home game of the year. They responded like true champions always do.

While the usual suspects all came to play, it was Andre Iguodala that stood out amongst the crowd and was the best player on the floor in Game Six. Iguodala controlled the game from the opening tip and by the time the third quarter ended he had already registered a triple double with 13 points, 11 rebounds and 10 assists to go along with 4 steals and 2 blocks.

Your Celtics entered the fourth quarter with a 84-76 lead and the game seemingly in control ... then Kevin Durant caught fire. Durant buried five three-pointers and scored 19 points to lead the Thunder to an improbable 106-102 lead with just 39 seconds remaining in the game. After a layup by Gordon Hayward, followed by a missed three-pointer by Russell Westbrook that would have iced the game for the Thunder but was an ill-advised shot attempt, the Celtics found themselves down 106-104 with just 17 seconds remaining.

After a full timeout by Coach Brad Stevens the Celtics took the floor and Gordon Hayward calmly inbounded the ball to Andre Iguodala for what looked to be a typical isolation play. Iguodala had been magnificent the entire game, passing like a wizard and rebounding like a warrior as usual, but also being able to score almost at will on the unusually poor defense of Kevin Durant, to the tune of 20 points on just 11 shot attempts.

After receiving the inbounds pass Iguodala and Goran Dragic played hot potato a couple times before Iguodala held the ball for 2-3 seconds to let the clock run down to just 8 seconds; when the clock hit 8 Iggy attacked. The uber-athletic small forward blew by Kevin Durant on his way to the basket; however as he made his way into the paint he realized he could either attempt an extremely difficult floater over Serge Ibaka or use his body as a shield and try to draw a foul with little hope of making the layup attempt.

Iguodala chose to try and draw a foul but while he was taking his final dribble towards the basket Gordon Hayward was quickly yet quietly drifting to the three-point line and away from the defense of Thabo Sefolosha. Iguodala spotted a wide-open Hayward out of the corner of his eye and fired a perfect pass just a split-second before he was about to leap and undoubtedly crash into Ibaka. Hayward caught Iguodala's perfect pass with just 4 seconds on the clock, feigned a quick pass to Goran Dragic to freeze the defense ... and then let fly. The ball swished through the net as the buzzer sounded and Hayward's arms raised triumphantly for all to see.

Your Celtics won the series penultimate game 107-106 due in large part to the all-around dominance of Andre Iguodala who finished with 20 points, 13 assists and 15 rebounds. The series was knotted at 3 games apiece and headed back to Chesapeake Energy Arena in Oklahoma City for a decisive Game Seven.

Going into Game Seven, most talking heads felt the series would end with Kevin Durant holding both the *Larry O'Brien Championship Trophy* as well as the *Bill Russell NBA Finals Most Valuable Player Award*. Russell Westbrook had played fantastic basketball through-out the series, averaging 25.5 points, 7.5 assists and 5.5 rebounds while Celtics stars Kevin Love (26.5 points and 12.5 rebounds) Goran Dragic (20.5 points and 9.0 assists), and Omer Asik (13.5 points, 13.5 rebounds and 2.0 blocks) had all played magnificent basketball. However, it was the man known as the *Durantula* who had given the most virtuoso performances on a consistent basis, entered Game Seven averaging a remarkable 28.5 points, 7.5 rebounds and 5.5 assists per game, and seemed ready to ascend to the top of the NBA's current Mount Rushmore.

Though the series was knotted at 3 games apiece the Thunder had outscored your Celtics 644-573, or by an average of 11.8 points per game through the first 6 games of the series, and the consensus in Vegas was that the Thunder would win Game Seven by at least 12 points. Even Larry Bird himself stated, *I'm afraid that unless Kevin Love can drop 50 and Kevin Durant can't buy a bucket, the Thunder are going to win this title.*

NBA Finals Game Seven: When Game Seven began the Celtics starting five of Goran Dragic, Gordon Hayward, Andre Iguodala, Kevin Love and Omer Asik refused to acknowledge their Oklahoma City Thunder counterparts whatsoever, which made for an awkward scene and seemed to catch the Thunder players off-guard. Kevin Durant seemed especially miffed when after he offered his hand to Love, who then waved him off with a disgusted snort and a rather homicidal glare.

After winning the opening tip the Celtics scored a quick bucket on a beautiful bounce pass from Dragic to Asik who flushed the ball through the hoop with unusual force, and then in an extremely uncharacteristic move, the Turkish big man let out a scream and stared down Kendrick Perkins who had tried to block the dunk. Referee Monty McCutchen slapped Asik with a technical foul and after Kevin Durant sunk the freebie the lines had been drawn and the battle was on.

The first quarter was an exercise in frantic aggression and offensive inefficiency and hearkened back to Game 7 of the 2010 NBA Finals between the Los Angeles Celtics and Boston Celtics. However, unlike that Game 7, your Celtics didn't find themselves with a 9 point lead at the end of the first 12 minutes but rather a 21-21 tie.

The second quarter was more of the same with each team's defense being more solid than its offense, though the Thunder offense did seem to be humming at a better clip than your Celtics. There were even two plays that left the crowd in hysterics. The first was an amazing half-court alley-oop from Russell Westbrook to Kevin Durant which Durant caught with his back to the basket and proceeded to bring the ball down to his knees before hammering it home in a move more suited to NBA 2K than a real NBA game. The second was a tip-dunk executed by Russell Westbrook. Jeremy Lamb had just taken a long jumper from the right baseline and as the ball caromed off the rim, into what seemed to be the waiting hands of Kevin Love, Westbrook came flying through the air from the left baseline, caught the ball with his right hand, quickly grabbed it with his left hand as well and then seemed to climb up the back of Love before slamming the ball with a remarkable amount of force, so much in fact that the crowd seemed almost shocked that the backboard didn't shatter.

When the second quarter buzzer sounded, the Thunder held a 46-42 lead, though both teams entered their respective locker rooms knowing this was anyone's game. The leading scorer, rebounder, dime-dropper, stealer and blocker for the Thunder was Kevin Durant, who despite turning the ball over four times already and missing all three of his three-point attempts had managed to score 13 points, pull down 7 rebounds, dish out 5 assists, swipe three passes and block 2 shots including one Avery Bradley dunk attempt. The Celtics attack was more varied with Kevin Love leading the team in scoring with 11 points, Omer Asik leading the team in rebounding with 10 boards, Goran Dragic leading the team in assists with 6, Gordon Hayward leading the team in steals with 2 and Andre Iguodala leading the team in blocks with 2, including a come-from-behind block on a Thabo Sefolosha layup attempt at the end of the first half.

Back in the Celtics locker room Coach Brad Stevens implored his team to continue playing tough defense, not to give an inch of breathing room to Kevin Durant or Russell Westbrook, and above all else, not to give up any easy layups. When backup small forward Francisco Garcia said, *Coach, the refs are on OKC's side. If I even touch one of the Thunder with my pinkie-finger they're blowing the whistle. I feel like we're playing 5-on-8 out there and will need a miracle to win.* Coach Stevens then lit into Garcia and the entire team saying, *I don't care about the refs, you let me deal with the refs. All I care about is you making life miserable on the Thunder. I don't want to see them get even one easy layup in the second half, not one. If you're a backup, like you are Francisco, I'd rather see you guys get ejected after blowing up a Thunder player who thinks he's going to get an easy layup than just watch the ball drop through the hoop trying to avoid the foul. Don't forget men, I coached Butler to back-to-back NCAA Finals; Butler! Ask a normal fan who Butler is and they'll probably tell you 'he's the old guy who looks after Batman'. I am a great coach, not a good coach, a great coach and I'm telling you guys right now, you are a great team, a greater team than OKC is and we are going to win this game! Now, go out there and shock the world!*

Your Celtics took the court in the third quarter ready for Armageddon. Just four minutes into the third and it was obvious Francisco Garcia took Coach Stevens' words to heart as much as a Biblical Christian takes the words of Christ to heart. Jeremy Lamb had beat Gordon Hayward on a back-door cut and was gliding in for an easy uncontested layup when Garcia came crashing into him.

When the two tumbled to the floor Lamb gave Garcia and elbow and Francisco responded with one of his own. The two players continued to tussle before being separated by the referees and ultimately thrown out of the game for striking each other. Needless to say, the loss of starting shooting guard Lamb was a far greater blow to the Thunder than was the loss of backup small forward Garcia to the Celtics. The Celtics took advantage of Lamb's ejection and outscored the Thunder

27-23 in the third quarter, tying the game at 69 apiece heading into the final quarter of the final game of the 2014-15 season.

While both Coach Brooks and Coach Stevens usually started fourth quarters with their starters getting some much needed rest on the bench, each coach decided to let their starters play the entire fourth quarter in this do-or-die game. The only exception was OKC's Jeremy Lamb who was replaced by Thabo Sefolosha after his ejection.

The fourth quarter was filled with fireworks, both on the court and on the sidelines, with each team's respective coach picking up a technical foul during the first eight minutes of the quarter. However, each team rose to the challenge, competed as if their lives depended on the outcome and executed their offense beautifully, while at the same time playing tough, mistake-free defense.

With just four minutes remaining in the game the Thunder held a 93-90 lead thanks in large part to Russell Westbrook's nine fourth quarter points. Over the next 3:15 of game time the Celtics and Thunder each scored six points with Russell Westbrook hitting two more three-pointers (giving him 15 points in the fourth quarter and 30 points for the game) and Goran Dragic nailing one three-pointer, with Kevin Love converting on one incredibly difficult three point play (giving him a team-leading 29 points for the game).

After a quick steal by Andre Iguodala off an inbounds pass, and yet another layup by Goran Dragic cut the Thunder lead to 99-98 with 29 seconds remaining, Thunder Coach Scott Brooks called a timeout to set up the play he hoped would win him the title. On the Celtics side-line Coach Stevens held the team's full attention. He told the team he was positive, absolutely positive that the Thunder were going to use Kevin Durant as a decoy and distributor on their final play and that they were going to the on-fire Russell Westbrook for their final shot.

Coach Stevens took Gordon Hayward out of the game and inserted Avery Bradley and also instructed Avery Bradley to guard Thabo Sefolosha but to give him a solid cushion as he was sure Sefolosha would not be receiving the ball in this situation, and that even if he did, there is no way he would actually shoot it. He instructed Bradley to immediately double Russell Westbrook the second he catches the ball, even if that meant leaving Sefolosha wide open. Andre Iguodala was assigned to Kevin Durant while Kevin Love was assigned to Serge Ibaka and Omer Asik was assigned to Steven Adams with instructions to box out like crazy.

Just as Coach Stevens thought, the Thunder inbounded the ball to Kevin Durant at the top of the key for what looked to be an isolation play. Durant held the ball until there was just 10 seconds left on the shot clock before making his move towards the basket. Durant dribbled to his right, tucked his head and started a foray into the line. Iguodala was draped on Durant like a blanket however and before Durant got into the paint, he stopped, gave one quick pump fake and then fired a pass to the right baseline for Russell Westbrook who had just come off a screen set by Steven Adams and broken free from the defense of Goran Dragic.

By the time Westbrook caught Durant's pass and turned to face the basket Dragic had recovered and was in position to challenge the shot. Avery Bradley had also left Sefolosha just as Coach Stevens had instructed him to do and was sneakily making his way towards Westbrook as well.

Westbrook then gave a dribble towards the right baseline before executing a lightning fast spin back towards the middle of the court, followed by one more dribble to his left and then elevating to shoot a fade-away jump-shot. However, just as the ball left his finger-tips, Bradley's outstretched hand swatted the ball out of bounds, but before the ball landed Iguodala leapt and batted the ball back inbounds to Omer Asik who quickly called time out with just 9 seconds remaining in the game and the Celtics trailing 99-98.

During the time out, Coach Stevens gathered his troops and simply said, *Give the ball to Goran and get out of the way; and Goran, make the right play. Goran Dragic responded by saying, Don't worry coach, I got this. Gordon, float to the three-point line; Omer and Iggy, crash the boards; Kevin, let's play some pick and roll big fella.*

When the Celtics took the floor they noticed Russell Westbrook was nowhere to be found. It seemed he had rolled his ankle on the last shot attempt and was icing it on the bench. The Thunder had Kevin Durant guarding Dragic, second year wing-man and athletic freak Andre Roberson guarding Gordon Hayward, Thabo Sefolosha guarding Andre Iguodala, Serge Ibaka guarding Kevin Love and Kendrick Perkins guarding Omer Asik. No matter, Dragic was getting the ball.

As soon as Goran Dragic caught Iguodala's inbound pass, Kevin Durant was in his face. Dragic calmly held the ball for two seconds, time enough for Kevin Love to set a screen just inside the three-point line at the center of the court. Dragic rolled to his right and used Love's pick to get into the lane. As he reached the right side of the lane, Serge Ibaka left Kevin Love to come double Dragic. Dragic then spun quickly to his left, splitting the Durant and Ibaka double-team, took one more dribble towards the rim, gave a quick head-fake and began to spin once again to attempt a fade away jumper from just inside the free-throw line.

However, just before Dragic was about to elevate he saw Andre Roberson leave Gordon Hayward and charge towards him, obviously with the intention of blocking his jump-shot. Dragic waited a split second, did a 180' spin … and then … just as Roberson leaped towards him, threaded a beautiful bounce pass between and under the legs of Zeller to a wide-open Gordon Hayward who let fly from just inside the arc.

Hayward's shot swished through the net as time expired. Chesapeake Energy Arena went dead-silent.

The Celtics bench emptied in celebration. Your Celtics, the team whose roster you built, the team whose trade's you executed, your Celtics won the NBA Championship!

NBA Commission Adam Silver presented Celtics CEO Wyc Grousbeck with the *Larry O'Brien Championship Trophy*. Bill Russell stood by the platform ready to present the *Bill Russell NBA Finals Most Valuable Player Award*.

Kevin Love finished the Finals averaging 26.0 points, and 12.0 rebounds while shooting a magnificent .549 from the floor, while Goran Dragic finished the series averaging 20.0 points, 8.6 assists, 4.4 rebounds and 2.0 steals. Both players were worthy of winning Finals MVP.

Commissioner Silver motioned for the great Bill Russell to make his way to the stage while saying, *In the history of the NBA Finals there has never been Co-MVP's ... until now. I'm pleased to present this award to Co-MVP's Kevin Love of the Boston Celtics and Kevin Durant of the Oklahoma City Thunder. Kevin Durant becomes just the second player from a losing team in league history to win this award while Kevin Love wins this award for the first time in his brief yet remarkable career. Each superstar played magnificent basketball throughout this epic series. Congratulations to both Kevin Love and Kevin Durant, two deserving NBA Finals Most Valuable Players!*

EXIT MEETING WITH WYC GROUSBECK

Celtics CEO Wyc Grousbeck: *You did it baby, you did it! You took over one of the worst teams and lineups in the league and turned it into an NBA champion in one year!*

You have proven yourself to be a veritable basketball genius, a General Manager mastermind! I always knew I hired the right person for this job. There were a couple times where I questioned you but I never lost faith that you would get the job done, and that's exactly what you did!

You're an NBA champion and I want you to know that if you want to be here, I want you here. I know there are a lot of teams out there that will offer you the moon to come and rescue their team and take over as GM, but those teams aren't the Boston Celtics, your Boston Celtics!

All I can say is congratulations and I hope you will sign a long-term extension with us. Great job champ!

EPILOGUE

Writing this book has been a blast and I hope you enjoyed reading it as much as I enjoyed writing it. There aren't many sports fans on the planet that have been blessed with the ability to write such a book as this, the free time needed to complete such a project as this and the loving and understanding wife and children necessary to support one's dedication to such a work as this. I am a blessed man.

I know that not all fans will agree with the course one must follow in this book in order to win the NBA title. I imagine there are many readers who feel that Rajon Rondo should never be traded and deserves to retire as a Celtic, or that someone like the Milwaukee Bucks Larry Sanders would be a better option to acquire in trade than Omer Asik. There may even be many readers out there who feel that it's realistic to believe the LeBron James would sign with the Celtics if given the chance and that I should have written that option into the storyline, despite all reason and logic saying otherwise.

The point of this book is not to set forth the most perfect plan the Celtics should follow this summer, as in reality such may be building for the future and not trying to win a title immediately at all, for as any fan knows two titles in 10 years is better than one title immediately with none to follow in the next nine years. Rather, this book is merely meant as a fun exercise in armchair General Management and nothing more. However, I will say that if the goal is to win a title *this season*, the future be damned, than the plan this book outlines is perhaps better than any other floating around in the ether at this time, period.

It's fun to read articles about what could have been such as hindsight drafts. For example, it's fun to think about how Michael Jordan's and for that matter Clyde Drexler's careers would have played out had Jordan been drafted by the Portland Trailblazers instead of Sam Bowie. Would Jordan have scored far less career points and won less individual trophies but even more rings than he did in Chicago? Would Drexler have been willing to play Robin to Jordan's Batman or would chemistry issues have caused the team to go ring-less while the two players were on the same roster? What if Jordan would have been drafted #1 overall in the 1984 draft as he should have been and Hakeem Olajuwon been drafted second by the Portland Trailblazers to team with Drexler? Would Jordan be ring-less and Hakeem and Clyde sitting pretty on an NBA Mount Rushmore list with six rings apiece?

Thinking about what could have transpired if a team would or wouldn't have made a particular trade is also a fun mental exercise. For example, what would have happened had Kobe Bryant not used his no-trade-clause and vetoed the agreement Dr. Jerry Buss had to send the then 3-time champion to the Detroit Pistons for Rip Hamilton, Tayshaun Prince, Amir Johnson and a first round pick? Would the Lakers still be looking for their first post Kobe& Shaq title? Would Kobe have seven rings by now with four coming as a Piston thereby topping

Michael Jordan's six titles and assuring that Kobe would one day enter the Hall of Fame as a Piston rather than a Laker?

The possibilities are almost endless when it comes to thinking about the what-could-have-been in sports and thinking about what could have been can be extremely fun, or in the case of many Celtics fans who have pondered what-could-have-been with Len Bias and Reggie Lewis, heart-breaking. However, the fun one can have thinking about what could have been actually pales in comparison to the fun one can have thinking about what could be in the future, as such mere thoughts could still become reality.

Becoming a sports seer or basketball prophet would be an insanely enjoyable way to earn a living. Writing this book allowed me to become such for a time and it would be great to see this book spark an entirely new genre of sports fiction: *Be the General Manager.*

Readers of all ages have loved *Choose Your Own Adventure* books since the idea was first conceived by Princeton University and Columbia Law School graduate Edward Packard. Packard's first title was *Sugarcane Island* which was released in 1976 as an *Adventures of You* series published by Vermont Crossroads Press. Bantam Books started publishing the *Choose Your Own Adventure* series shortly thereafter selling more than 250,000,000 copies between 1979 (the year I was born) and 1998 (the year after I married my high school sweetheart and our first child was conceived).I think it's high time *Be the General Manager* books become every bit as popular!

APPENDIX THREE:
LEBRON JAMES' NEW DECISION

Many readers may wonder why LeBron James plays for the Cleveland Cavaliers and not the Miami Heat in this book. The answer to this question is two-fold.

Firstly, this is my book and if I want to write LeBron onto the Cavs rather than the Heat, onto the Cavs he shall go. Secondly, I honestly believe that if the Miami Heat do not three-peat as NBA Champions this season, there is a solid 55% chance LeBron will bolt South Beach and take his talents back to Cleveland – *at least we're not Detroit* – Ohio.

Would LeBron James really leave the shores of Biscayne Bay for the shores of the Cuyahoga River? Would he really trade the fun and sun of Miami for the snow, slush and sullenness of Cleveland? If such a trade would mean winning even one more ring over the remainder of his career, than I believe the answer is yes!

The man known as *King James* has a new decision to make this summer. However, he has already proven that he marches to the beat of his own drummer, that he does not care what his critics say, and that winning titles and increasing his personal legacy while building his individual *brand* are far more important to him than is loyalty to any one NBA franchise (and rightly so I might add).

James left Cleveland for Miami, not because Micky Arison was a better owner than Dan Gilbert or because Eric Spoelstra was a better coach than Mike Brown. He switched teams simply because he thought he could win more titles over the length of his next contract with the Heat than he could with the Cavs, period.

The above said, it stands to reason that this summer, when LeBron takes stock of his future and the probably futures of other teams around the league with him on their roster, he won't have a problem switching teams once again, if doing so will give him better odds at winning multiple titles. I personally believe joining the Cleveland Cavaliers would do just that.

Now, before I explain why leaving Miami for Cleveland makes too much sense for LeBron to ignore, I would like to touch on two apparent truths:

Firstly, I do believe if the Miami Heat three-peat this season, there is at least an 80 percent chance LeBron either picks up his *player option* or signs an extension and plays at least one more season with the Heat. Even if LeBron believes Wade is washed up and that Bosh is little more than a third option at this stage of his career when he truly needs a second option, I believe LeBron will return to Miami. I just cannot fathom how he could turn down the possibility, even if such is remote, of winning four-straight NBA titles with Miami, thereby accomplishing a feat Michael Jordan never did. LeBron wants to ascend to the top of the NBA's mythical Mount Rushmore and he knows that he needs to top Jordan, more so than any other single player, to do so.

Secondly, while most talking heads seem to feel the only team LeBron would even consider leaving the Heat for is the Cavaliers, I do believe that LeBron would consider other options if he felt such would help him win more titles than a move to Cleveland would bring. I also have no doubt in my mind that every single NBA team would willing move mountains to make it possible for LeBron to sign with them and that the only player in the entire league who's team would not trade him for LeBron, or to make room for LeBron, is 2013-14 NBA *MVP* Kevin Durant.

The above said, it would not shock me all that much to see LeBron James tell the Clippers he will ink a maximum contract with them, with a starting salary of $20,020,875 if they can open up a roster spot for him while at the same time keeping Chris Paul and Blake Griffin on the roster. However, as I don't believe the Miami Heat would agree to trade LeBron to another team and that they would in fact dare him to simply sign with another team, and as the trio of James, Paul and Griffin would be on the books for $57,722,126 all by themselves, leaving just $4,377,874 to spend on a minimum of nine other players which is less than even nine minimum contract salaries would account for, such is an impossibility, unless James decides to take a pay-cut and accept less than the maximum. I don't see that happening.

By the way, the above should tell the reader something, namely that many of the talking heads on sports shows around the country, have literally no idea what they are talking about when they talk about free agency signings and trades. During the 2013-14 season there was a *report* that Carmelo Anthony to the Clippers was a very realistic possibilty. When I heard that I laughed and knew that whoever first came up with such a ridiculous idea and whichever reports foolishly chose to report on such, each did so in complete ignorance and without any legitimate understanding of the salary cap, trade financial and the NBA's *Collective Bargaining Agreement*.

The simple fact is that due to Carmelo Anthony's previous contract with the Knicks being more lucrative than the previous contract LeBron James signed with the Heat, Anthony can earn a higher maximum salary than James this offseason. If it would be impossible for the Clippers to pair James with Chris Paul and Blake Griffin, it would be even more impossible for them to pair Anthony with the two Los Angeles stars. Simply put, take what you hear on sports broadcasts and news networks with a grain of salt, at least when it comes to free agency and trade rumors and gossip.

Back to LeBron and his new decision. While James may not be able to force his way to the Los Angeles Clippers or New York Knicks (who would need to find a team willing to absorb the contracts of both Amare Stoudemire and Andrea Bargnani if they wanted to team LeBron with Carmelo Anthony and a decent title-worthy roster), there is one team that I know James could join, would love to join, would love to have him join, and while such a team also may give James the greatest chance to win multiple titles, probably is an extreme long-shot. I am speaking of Kevin Durant's Oklahoma City Thunder!

I remember watching an NBA pre-game show with my son this season and Bill Simmons stating the Thunder would easily win the West if they would just trade Perkins and Lamb for the Orlando Magic's Aaron Afflalo. Now, don't get me wrong, I love *The Sports Guy* and think he's a genius writer and one of the best talking heads in the business, but his statement was just silly and akin to saying, t*he Golden State Warriors would easily win the title if they would just trade Iggy and Barnes for LeBron* – of course they would, but it takes two teams to sign off on a trade – unless you're playing NBA2K.

The Magic would never agree to trade Afflalo for the horrendous *should have been amnestied* contract of Kendrick Perkins simply to land Jeremy Lamb; word is that they refused to swap Afflalo for Eric Bledsoe (who is in an entirely different stratosphere as a player than Jeremy Lamb) before the season started and if they did want to dump Afflalo they could get a whole lot more than Perkins and Lamb.

However, when Bill Simmons stated the Thunder needed to make a trade it got me thinking … what would have happened had Magic and Bird played together? What about Russell and Chamberlain? How about Shaq and Kobe;

oh yeah, we know the answer to this last one, 3 NBA titles and 4 Conference championships in 5 years!

The above said, we all know LeBron had no problem signing with *Dwyane Wade's team* simply because he felt doing so gave him the greatest chance to win multiple rings. Of course he quickly turned the Heat into *LeBron's team* but the point is that he didn't mind signing with a team that already had a face of the franchise and beloved team leader. That said, what one player do you think LeBron feels could help him win the most rings possible? Kevin Durant of course!

If LeBron James tells the Thunder this summer, *I want to sign with you and play with K.D.*, not only will they move mountains to get him, they could actually do so very, very easily. Let me make this very clear, the Oklahoma City Thunder could easily make room to sign LeBron James to a max contract this summer, and, that hat is a horrifying thought for the rest of the NBA!

All the Thunder brass would need to do would be to trade the duo of Jeremy Lamb and Nick Collison for a future pick, which they could easily do, and trade Russell Westbrook for future picks as well, and obviously they would have no trouble doing that at all. There are probably upwards of 20 NBA franchises that would fall all over themselves to hand the Thunder first round draft picks from now through the next 6 years for Westbrook if they could.

Once the Thunder brass accomplished those two simple moves, they could pick up the team option on little-used but intriguing giant Hasheem Thabeet, sign five minimum level contract players and roll out the following title-ready roster to start the 2014-15 NBA season:

Starting Point Guard:	Reggie Jackson	$2,325,680
Starting Shooting Guard:	Kevin Durant	$19,997,513
Starting Small Forward:	LeBron James	$20,020,875
Starting Power Forward:	Serge Ibaka	$12,250,000
Starting Center:	Steven Adams	$2,184,960

Backup Point Guard:	Minimum Contract Player	
Backup Shooting Guard:	Minimum Contract Player	
Backup Small Forward:	Andre Roberson	$773,920
Backup Power Forward:	Perry Jones	$1,129,200
Backup Center:	Hasheem Thabeet	$1,250,000
11th Man:	Minimum Contract Player	
12th Man:	Minimum Contract Player	
13th Man:	Minimum Contract Player	

I don't know about you but that starting five would scare the pants off me, no matter which team I was in charge of! Now, I will say that I do not believe LeBron James will force his way to the Thunder, nor do I believe he would even seriously consider playing for the Thunder and with frenemy and arch-rival Kevin Durant … unless … both the Heat and Thunder fail to win the 2014 NBA title.

If the Heat win this season's title I believe LeBron will return to Miami for at least one more season. If the Thunder win the title I believe LeBron could bolt Miami, but not that he would join the current champion in Oklahoma. However, if a team like the Indiana Pacers or San Antonio Spurs win this year's title, I could most definitely see LeBron seriously considering teaming up with Kevin Durant in Oklahoma and forming the great dynasty the league has seen since the Bill Russell led Celtics!

Now, as *En Vogue*, and one of the most amazing looking women God ever created other than my wife, Cindy Herron, would say, *back to life, back to reality*. It's now time to get back to explaining why leaving Miami for Cleveland makes too much sense for LeBron James to ignore:

The Miami Heat are cap-strapped, period. After Dwyane Wade, Chris Bosh and LeBron himself all exercise their player options for the 2014-15 season, those three salaries combined with nothing more than the inexpensive salaries of Chris *Birdman* Anderson and Norris Cole, place the Heat nearly $3,000,000 over the salary cap, with just five players under contract.

Just about the best thing the Miami brass can hope for is for all of their 2013-14 roster players to agree to re-sign, preferably at massive hometown discounts. Even if such happens, which is a long-shot, especially considering starting point guard Mario Chalmers may be looking for a sizeable raise and youngsters Michael Beasley and Greg Oden may desire to play for a team that will actually allow them to play the game of basketball outside of practice, the Heat will merely trot out a more aged and broken down version of their 2013-14 season. Such a roster certainly does not guarantee a title going forward and may not even be one of the four of five best rosters when the 2014-15 season rolls around.

However, over in Cleveland, the Cavs not only have a superstar point guard in Kyrie Irving. They have a 22 year old superstar point guard and a player that could be dominating the competition at a time when both Dwyane Wade and Chris Bosh are enjoying retirement. Irving, in and of himself, is reason enough for LeBron James to seriously consider a bolt back to Cleveland.

The Cavaliers also have 2013 #1 Draft Pick Anthony Bennett, a player who may have disappointed in his rookie season, but one with immense potential nonetheless, and yet another player that may be dominating the completion at a time when both Wade and Bosh are sipping drinks on a Miami Beach and enjoying their retirement. The 21 year old *tweener* actually had a very solid 10 game stint during the middle of his rookie season that started with his first career *double-double* and ended with a solid 15 point, 8 rebound performance. During the 10 games Bennett actually managed to average 16.5 points and 10.2 rebounds per 40 minutes while also knocking down seven three-pointers at a .412 clip, showing his potential as a dynamic *stretch-four* type of forward.

Cleveland also has a pair of #4 overall picks in 23 year old power forward Tristan Thompson and 22 year old shooting guard Dion Waiters. Both players are loaded with potential, and, just as with Irving and Bennett, could be starring in the league at a time when Dwyane Wade and Chris Bosh are playing NBA2K and wishing they were still in the league. Thompson is a double-double waiting to happen (career averages of close to 15 points and 12 rebounds per 40 minutes) while Waiters is a dynamic scorer (career average of nearly 21 points per 40 minutes) who was actually compared to Wade leading up to the 2012 NBA Draft.

The Cavs also have two other recently drafted youngsters on the books with cheap rookie scale contracts. Tyler Zeller, the 17th pick in the 2012 NBA Draft and a player with career per 40 minute averages of around 13 points, 9 rebounds and 1.4 blocks. And, Sergey Karasev, the 19th pick in the 2013 NBA Draft and a sweet shooting small forward from Russia.

Oh yeah, and they also won the Draft Lottery this past May 20th and have the number one overall pick in this June's upcoming draft as well. Whether they draft Joel Embiid, Andrew Wiggins or Jabari Parker, or simply trade the pick for an available superstar like Kevin Love, the simple fact is the Cavaliers are loaded, absolutely loaded!

The only other player Cleveland has *on the books* for the 2014-15 season is back-up point guard Jarrett Jack. Jack is a steady 30 year old combo guard, who despite having a bit of an off year this season, managed to average 9.6 points and 4.0 assists per game with a 2.35-to-1 assist-to-turnover ratio in just over 28 minutes per game.

The above said, if the Cavaliers were to sign LeBron James this summer to a maximum contract with a starting salary of $20,020,875 and draft and sign two rookies with their first and second round (via the Orlando Magic) draft picks, who for the sake of listing players in the following roster rather than just saying *Draft Pick*, I'll say Joel Embiid and Glenn Robinson III with the first and thirty-third overall picks, their roster would look as follows:

Starting Point Guard:	Kyrie Irving	$7,459,924
Starting Shooting Guard:	Dion Waiters	$4,062,000
Starting Small Forward:	LeBron James	$20,020,875
Starting Power Forward:	Trist. Thompson	$5,421,233
Starting Center:	Joel Embiid	$5,510,640

Backup Point Guard:	Jarrett Jack	$6,300,000
Backup Shooting Guard:	Sergey Karasev	$1,533,840
Backup Small Forward:	Anthony Bennett	$5,563,920
Backup Power Forward:	Free Agent – up to	$4,609,136
Backup Center:	Tyler Zeller	$1,703,760
11th Man:	Glenn Robinson	$507,336
12th Man:	Minimum Contract Player	

The ten players above would combine to earn $63,200,000 and therefore Cavaliers brass would indeed have up to $4,609,136 to spend on one free agent. This said, the team could sign one minimum player such as an undrafted rookie free agent like Iowa State's combo guard DeAndre Kane for example, and then use the remaining $4,609,136 to re-sign longtime Cavalier Anderson Varejao, whom they would have previously declined their team option on as he is no longer worth his scheduled salary. They could then sign one more minimum contract veteran, perhaps shooting guard and long-range bomber Anthony Morrow (if he chooses not to exercise his 2014-15 player option) and enter the 2014-15 season with the following roster:

Starting Point Guard:	Kyrie Irving
Starting Shooting Guard:	Dion Waiters
Starting Small Forward:	LeBron James
Starting Power Forward:	Tristan Thompson
Starting Center:	Joel Embiid
Backup Point Guard:	Jarrett Jack
Backup Shooting Guard:	Anthony Morrow
Backup Small Forward:	Anthony Bennett
Backup Power Forward:	Anderson Varejao
Backup Center:	Tyler Zeller
11th Man:	Glenn Robinson

12th Man: Sergey Karasev

13th Man: DeAndre Kane

The Miami Heat simply cannot match, let alone top, the above lineup. They cannot legitimately surround LeBron with four 25 year old and under quality starters. They cannot surround LeBron with a roster that could realistically remain together and dominant for the next decade.

The Heat can offer LeBron an aged and experienced roster while the Cavs can offer LeBron a potential-laced roster filled with young stars. The Heat can offer LeBron a great shot at winning perhaps one more ring. The Cavs can offer LeBron a great shot at being in contention for a ring for the next 10 seasons.

I will say one final time. If the Heat win the 2013-14 title I do believe LeBron will play at least one more season in Miami. If they fail to do so I believe LeBron will seriously consider bolting to Cleveland. And, I for one, believe Cleveland offers LeBron a better chance at winning multiple rings over the next decade than Miami does, period.

PRINT BOOK BONUS APPENDIX

From: Bryant T. Jordan

Author of: *Saving the Lakers: A Be the General Manager Book*, *Saving the Celtics: A Be the General Manager Book* and *An Open Letter to ALL Regarding Donald Sterling*

Email: author@bryantTjordan.com

To: Cleveland Cavaliers General Manager David Griffin

Dear Mr. Griffin,

Please consider the following:

Cavaliers Trade:	2014 #1 Pick, Tristan Thompson, Anthony Bennett and Jarrett Jack
Raptors Trade:	Demar DeRozan, Jonas Valaciunas, 2014 #20 pick and the expiring contract of Dwight Buycks

Why the Raptors Agree:

Andrew Wiggins belongs on the Toronto Raptors, to play his entire career with the Raptors, to retire a Raptor and to be the first (and perhaps only) player to have his jersey hanging from the rafters and number retired. That the Raptors would also be acquiring talented and potential-filled *Canadians* in Anthony Bennett and Tristan Thompson – both of which are players that I believe would not only agree to contract extensions down the line but actually desire to sign such extensions with the Raptors more so than with any other team in the league – is a great plus as well; a great plus that Raptors General Manager Masai Ujiri should appreciate a great deal.

I sincerely believe that Andrew Wiggins, Tristan Thompson and Anthony Bennett will not only be ecstatic to be traded to the Toronto Raptors, but that they will be ecstatic to stay with the Raptors for the remainder of their careers. And, as I also believe that all three will most likely be playing for the *Canadian Olympic Team* in the 2016, 2020, 2024 Olympics and on, the chemistry of a team lead by such players could be San Antonio Spurs-esque.

In regards to Jarrett Jack, he is a quality backup combo guard and if the Raptors happen to lose Kyle Lowry to free agency, Jack would be a capable veteran starter on a young team lead by *The Canadian Three* of Wiggins, Thompson and

Bennett, along with talented swingman Terrence Ross. And, if Lowry happens to re-sign with the Raptors, Jack would be a great first guard off the bench.

The above said, I believe my trade proposal is not only a no-brainer trade for the Toronto Raptors franchise, the Raptors faithful fans, the city of Toronto, the Province of Ontario and for Canada as a country; I believe it's a no-brainer trade for General Manager Masai Ujiri as well. He can cement his place in Canadian lore by pulling off this trade and that is why YOU Mr. Griffin, need to strike while the iron's hot, and pull off this deal NOW!

Why the Cavaliers Agree:

I believe you're intelligent enough to recognize my trade proposal as a no-brainer, in the same way I believe Lakers General Manager Mitch Kupchak was intelligent enough to recognize my January, 2008 trade proposal of Kwame Brown, Javaris Crittenton, Marc Gasol, picks and cash for Pau Gasol; a trade (with the addition of Aaron Mckie) that Kupchak did in fact pull off, and which led to the Lakers 3-peating as Western Conference champions and winning two more NBA titles as well. However, please indulge me and allow me to write my piece.

I recognize that one of the most difficult aspects of being the General Manager of the Cleveland Cavaliers and building a perennial title-contender in Cleveland is the stigma that Cleveland is a small – and cold – market. It's one thing to draft a star prospect or even trade for a star talent, and yet an entirely different thing to keep such a talent locked up for the long-term. The tortured Cleveland fans know this better than anyone. That said, I believe you have one of the most difficult jobs in the league as you not only have to build a title-contender, you have to do so in a market that many players don't respect or appreciate. For example, you may be able to offer a wonderful trade package for a star player such as Kevin Love, only to watch him play for nothing more than his next contract, and then bolt Cleveland as soon as the 2014-15 season ends, in order to sign with a big market team like the Lakers or Knicks – even if LeBron

James does actually sign with the Cavaliers this summer. Kevin Love seems to have stars in his eyes and *winning* may not cure his wanderlust.

I also realize that LeBron James may not be ready to rejoin the Cavaliers with the current roster being what it is – even if a young star center like Joel Embiid is added to the mix. LaMarcus Aldridge isn't available. And, as for Kevin Love, I've explained my thoughts on him already.

However, the Toronto Raptors are ripe for the picking! There fan base is head over heels with Andrew Wiggins and Canadian *We are the North* pride is in full swing. If the fans get wind that the Cleveland Cavaliers have offered to trade the number one pick – and therefore their beloved Andrew Wiggins – along with two more young and talented Canadian players in Tristan Thompson and Anthony Bennett, they will be over the moon with excitement and demanding such a trade be completed. If Raptors General Manager Masai Ujiri does not pull the trigger on such a trade offer, the fans could be calling for his head – or at least his resignation since Canadians aren't as big on violence as Americans are – and demanding *Maple Leaf Sports and Entertainment* pull the trigger on the trade themselves.

As for the players themselves: DeMar DeRozan is a bona fide All-Star, just 24 years old and coming off a year where he was the 9th leading scorer in the NBA. However, as good as DeRozan is, Jonas Valanciunas may turn out to be even better. The big Lithuanian is just 22 years old and coming off a season in which he averaged 11 points and 9 boards and then upped his game in the playoffs by averaging 11 points and 10 boards while shooting over 63% from the field!

As for the #20 pick, it is also more valuable than ever this year, as the current draft crop is thought to be the deepest the league has seen since 1996 – at least that is my personal opinion - regardless of what the generally ingenious Jerry West thinks on the matter. As for the inclusion of the little-used Dwight Buycks, he is nothing more than a throw-in to *make financials work* of course.

When this deal and the NBA Draft is concluded, the Cavaliers will have just nine players *on the books*, including starters: Kyrie Irving, Dion Waiters, DeMar DeRozan, Jonas Valanciunas, and reserves: Tyler Zeller, Sergey Karasez, Dwight Buycks and whatever player they draft with the #20 pick (let's say Michigan State University power forward Adreian Payne) and the #33 pick (let's say Witchita State University swingman Cleyanthony Early) – and – the team will have also have $32,479,938 in available cap space. That's right, thirty-two million four hundred and seventy-nine thousand nine hundred and thirty-eight dollars in cap space!

With the aforementioned $32,479,938 in cap space your Cavaliers could literally offer LeBron James a maximum contract with a starting salary of $20,020,875, add one minimum contract veteran (let's say veteran point guard Devin Harris) to the roster, and still have $11,951,727 to spend on just one more starting big-man, while also being able to move Dion Waiters to the 6th man spot. With that $11,951,727 the Cavaliers could easily sign a big like Pau Gasol, Marcin Gortat or perhaps even Zach Randolph if the Grizzlies amnesty him, along with another quality free agent.

However, I personally believe if the Cavaliers *threw the house* – meaning all $11,951,727 of their remaining cap space – at the Detroit Pistons restricted free agent Greg Monroe in the form of a 4 year $51,033,874 contract, the Pistons may not match such a lucrative offer, and your Cavaliers could add one of the best young big men in the league to an already insanely potent roster. Such moves would give them a truly dynastic roster moving forward, a roster that would look as follows:

PG: Kyrie Irving

SG: DeMar DeRozan

SF: LeBron James

PF: Greg Monroe

C: Jonas Valanciunas

PG: Devin Harris

SG:	Dion Waiters
SF:	Cleanthony Early
PF:	Adreian Payne
C:	Tyler Zeller
11th Man:	Sergey Karasez
12th Man:	Dwight Buycks

Honestly, if LeBron James would rather play with the aging Dwyane Wade and Chris Bosh than with Kyrie Irving, DeMar DeRozan, Jonas Valanciunas *and* Greg Monroe, many will believe he is certifiably insane and ready for a padded room. LeBron James could literally own the NBA for the next decade playing with the above roster, a roster you would have built! By the time James' career winds down, he may not be chasing Michael Jordan's ring count, but Bill Russell's instead!

Now, just for the sake of argument – even if LeBron James doesn't return to Cleveland this summer (and if the Heat 3-Peat I don't think he will return to Cleveland, at least not before the 2015-16 season) and the Pistons decide to match the aforementioned 4 year $51,033,874 offer on Greg Monroe – your Cavaliers could still build a vastly improved roster by signing Carmelo Anthony in place of James, as well as the duo of Pau Gasol, and say, Andray Blatche in place of Greg Monroe, while also drafting point guard Elfrid Payton instead of power forward Adreian Payne with their #20 pick, and signing a veteran big like Emeka Okafor instead of Devin Harris to a minimum contract. Such moves would give the team the following roster to start next season:

PG:	Kyrie Irving
SG:	DeMar DeRozan
SF:	Carmelo Anthony
PF:	Pau Gasol
C:	Jonas Valanciunas

PG:	Elfrid Payton
SG:	Dion Waiters
SF:	Cleanthony Early
PF:	Andray Blatche
C:	Tyler Zeller
11th Man:	Emeka Okafor
12th Man:	Sergey Karasez
13th Man:	Dwight Buycks

The above roster is good enough to compete for a title immediately. More importantly, the above roster may be more than enough to lead tortured Cavaliers fans to consider you, David Griffin, a miracle worker, period. And, being considered a miracle worker can't be bad for an NBA General Manager these days.

Mr. Griffin, I believe if you contact Masai Ujiri, explain all of the above to him in your own words and work the ole *Griffin-magic*, you will be able to convince him to agree to such a trade and will be responsible for building the greatest roster in Cleveland Cavaliers history. In short, I believe you will be a legend!

Oh, and by the way, I won't even charge you a consulting fee. Just put me on the payroll after the Cavaliers win their first tilte, give me a massive cash bonus after they repeat and give me a lifetime consultant position after the 3-Peat.

Sincerely,

Bryant T. Jordan

Notes

Notes

Notes

ABOUT THE AUTHOR

Bryant T. Jordan is the author of *Saving the Lakers: A Be the General Manager Book* and *Saving the Celtics: A Be the General Manager Book*. He has been a freelance writer for over 15 years.

BTJ as many know him lives in a rural paradise with his high-school sweetheart and wife of 17 plus years, as well as his magnificent children, under the amazing care of His God and Savior. He considers himself the most blessed man on the planet, period.

You can generally find him leaving thought-proving tweets on Twitter @bryantTjordan

www.BryantTJordan.com

www.ingramcontent.com/pod-product-compliance
Lightning Source LLC
Chambersburg PA
CBHW060927040426

42445CB00011B/827

* 9 7 8 1 9 2 7 6 5 4 2 7 9 *